DADS

WHO STAY AND FIGHT

How to Be a **HERO**
for Your Family

DADS

WHO STAY AND FIGHT

How to Be a HERO
for Your Family

GREG TRIMBLE

CFI, an imprint of Cedar Fort, Inc.
Springville, Utah

ISBN 13: 978-1-4621-2004-8

Published by CFI, an imprint of Cedar Fort, Inc., 2373 W. 700 S., Springville, UT 84663
Distributed by Cedar Fort, Inc., www.cedarfort.com

LIBRARY OF CONGRESS CATALOGING-IN-PUBLICATION DATA
Library of Congress Cataloging-in-Publication Data

Names: Trimble, Greg, author.
Title: Dads who stay and fight : how to be a hero for your family / Greg
   Trimble.
Description: Springville, UT : CFI, an imprint of Cedar Fort, Inc., [2017] |
   Includes bibliographical references and index.
Identifiers: LCCN 2017000384 (print) | LCCN 2017006583 (ebook) | ISBN
   9781462120048 (pbk. : alk. paper) | ISBN 9781462127634 (e-book)
Subjects: LCSH: Fathers--Religious life. | Fatherhood--Religious
   aspects--Christianity. | Fatherhood--Religious aspects--Church of Jesus
   Christ of Latter-day Saints.
Classification: LCC BX8643.F3 T75 2017 (print) | LCC BX8643.F3 (ebook) | DDC
   248.8/421--dc23
LC record available at https://lccn.loc.gov/2017000384

Cover design by Kinsey Beckett
Cover design © 2017 by Cedar Fort, Inc.
Edited and typeset by Chelsea Holdaway

Printed in the United States of America

10 9 8 7 6 5 4 3 2 1

Printed on acid-free paper

*To every dad who wants to be
a hero for his family.*

CONTENTS

WHAT GOOD DADS DO

QUALITIES OF GOOD DADS

CONTENTS

DADS' ROLES

THE DAD RULES

SPIRITUAL DADS

CONTENTS

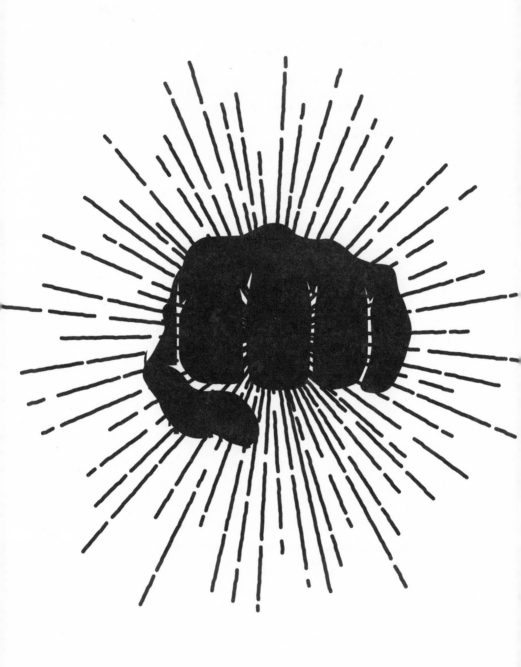

FOREWORD

Tim Ballard,
founder of Operation Underground Railroad
(O.U.R.)

SITTING IN AN old rented house in a Latin American country, my team and I worked to set up our next undercover sting operation. As I flipped through a catalog filled with faces of kids who have been taken and sold into slavery, I couldn't help but reflect on all the kids we've rescued in the past. It never gets any easier to look at the innocent little faces that have yet to be rescued.

The catalog I was looking at was used by traffickers to buy and sell kids, as if they were no better than a used car in an auto-trader magazine. While flipping through the pages, I pondered on the nearly seven hundred kids we've already been able to rescue from more than a dozen different countries. I was reminded that there are still so many kids out there who are literally living their worst nightmare—sold for a weekend escapade by these child traffickers. It's horrible, horrible stuff. We've encountered some of the most deplorable circumstances the human mind can conjure up.

Looking at the faces in the catalog, I knew what had led them into this, and almost all of them had a common story: no father in the child's life. A child was vulnerable and left to be taken because their father, who should have been their protector and provider, was gone. But there was one father who made all the difference for these rescued children: Guesno Mardy.

Guesno Mardy is a Haitian man who loved being a father to his son Gardy. Gardy was born in the United States during a fundraising mission, making him a US citizen, but he and his family lived in Haiti.

One Sunday, during a church meeting, Guesno sent Gardy across the congregation to find his mother, and then became distracted by another conversation. As Gardy made his way through the congregation, he was diverted and ultimately ended up walking toward the patio of the church, which led to the parking lot. It was there in the parking lot that a man grabbed Gardy, placed him on the back of a motorcycle, and sped off. That was the last time Guesno saw his son. Gardy was gone.

Guesno's life didn't get any easier after that. Two weeks after Gardy was taken, Guesno was talking to someone in the street outside of his office building. In that moment, the big Haiti earthquake hit. Guesno stood there and watched his two-story office building cave in on itself. His sister, brother-in-law, and close friend were inside: all died.

At that point, Guesno had an opportunity to move to the United States and take his remaining biological children with him. No one would have blamed him for leaving those horrific circumstances. But Guesno didn't want to leave his post as a father to more than 150 kids in his orphanage. He also didn't want to give up hope that he might find his son Gardy.

This is where I came in. When I learned about Guesno, I was an agent in the US government. When I read about his son Gardy, my heart went out to him. I thought to myself, "What is being done for this man?"

I wanted to know more about Guesno and his son, so I flew Guesno up to Utah. We met at Thanksgiving Point, and I asked him to tell me about everything he'd been going through.

"What's being done to find your son Gardy?" I asked. And before he answered my question, he asked me a question of his own that I didn't expect: "Do you have children?"

I said, "Yes, I do. I have six." (I had six at the time; I now have seven.)

Guesno then said to me, "Could you possibly sleep at night knowing that one of your children's beds was empty and you didn't know where they were?"

The very thought was impossible. "No, I could not," I responded.

In his humble voice, he said, "I have not slept since they took my son Gardy from me."

Then he proceeded to tell me (through tears—his tears and my tears), that every night, he gets up, arbitrarily picks some neighborhood in Port-au-Prince, and walks the streets with a flashlight, just hoping that somehow, someway, he will hear Gardy cry.

In that moment, my heart broke for Guesno; right then and there, I decided to change the direction of my life. I made a promise to Guesno that I would do everything in my power to help find Gardy.

Because Gardy was born in the US, I thought I could get the US government involved in finding Gardy. I wanted them to send me down to Haiti with a team and open up an investigation. But, there wasn't a strong enough connection to the United States to open up the investigation. I couldn't argue with their decision. This was purely a Haitian crime, not an American crime.

If I wanted to fulfill the promise I made to Guesno, I was going to have to make the scariest decision of my life. After lots of prayer and fasting and pondering, I made the crazy decision to leave one of the most secure jobs in the world—one that I loved—and leap out on my own. I left to start one of the most insecure companies: a non-profit organization, a company where you don't know when your next paycheck is coming in. But my team and I knew what we were supposed to do, and we felt like we were supposed to do it, so we did.

That was the beginning of Operation Underground Railroad (O.U.R.). We were going to save kids. And we were going to start in Haiti with Guesno and his son Gardy. As we arrived in Haiti, the Haitian National Police welcomed us in and gave us the backstory on the abduction of Gardy. We learned that through phone records and other information, the Haitian National Police were able to identify the person who had kidnapped this boy as a former employee of Guesno named Carlos. This same employee was working at the orphanage when he was caught embezzling money and was subsequently fired from his job. To get back at Guesno, Carlos made friends with some thugs and thought it was going to be a quick rip and ransom.

Carlos and the people who kidnapped Gardy assumed that Guesno was wealthy and demanded a $150,000 ransom. It was a ridiculous amount, and Guesno was only able to raise about $4,000. He gave all that he had for the ransom, yet Gardy was not returned to him. The traffickers let Carlos take the fall, and he was arrested. Gardy was never returned and was presumably placed into the traffickers network to be sold off for even more money.

Digging into the case, we found a connection between Carlos and a woman Carlos had communicated with while he was in prison. We figured we ought to pay a visit to her compound—a lot with big ten-foot cinder block walls. We suspected that this was a hub for child traffickers, or that she was in some way tied to them. Her building was disguised as an orphanage with a sign on the ten-foot walls that made it look like any other mom-and-pop orphanage in Haiti.

We decided to go in undercover and pose as American child traffickers. She opened up to us immediately, never suspecting that American cops would come to Haiti. She assumed that we knew her contacts and proceeded to offer us any one of the twenty-eight kids she had enslaved at her compound. $10,000 was the price per child.

At that point, we had her. We worked with the Haitian police to pull off a sting operation and take her place down. This woman and several others were arrested and locked up, and the twenty-eight children were rescued, but Gardy was nowhere to be found.

With a heavy heart, I met up with Guesno at a hotel to give him the results of our sting operation. As I approached him, I saw the hope and anticipation in his eyes. We sat down together, and I broke the news to him. It was a bittersweet moment. On the one hand, twenty-eight kids were freed from a most horrific future, but Gardy wasn't one of them.

Guesno put his head down, distraught at the loss of his son all over again. For ten or fifteen seconds, he mourned Gardy in agonized silence. But then, to my surprise, he popped up with a big smile on his face and asked, "What about the twenty-eight kids? Where are the twenty-eight kids?"

"Well . . . we got 'em. They're all safe. They're in good places," I told him.

Then Guesno said to me, "Do you realize that you never would have come down here and rescued those twenty-eight kids had it not been for my little Gardy?"

I said, "You're right."

Guesno then looked me in the eyes and said, "If I had to give up my son so that these twenty-eight kids could be rescued, then that's a burden I'm willing to bear." As he said those words, my mind was immediately taken to Christ, the Atonement, and the sacrifice of a loving Father.

I couldn't help but sit in awe of this great man—this humble man—who was enduring unimaginable heartache, yet displaying such divine character. If there was ever a modern representation of Job, I was sitting here in front of him.

Guesno is a dad who has taken his role as a father so seriously that he is unwilling to leave his post, give up, or run and hide, and is unwilling to wallow in the most excruciating grief a person can imagine. Mentally, he was able to give up his own flesh and blood, his precious two-year-old son, to be an instrument in rescuing others. He was so committed and firm in his resolve to be a father that he went down to the police department after learning about the twenty-eight rescued kids and said, "Bring them to me!" Guesno took in even more orphans, and literally became a father to the fatherless.

So, as I looked through that catalog of trafficked kids, I thought back on the hundreds of children that we've been fortunate enough to rescue over the years. I could see their faces. I could also envision the almost three hundred traffickers and pedophiles that we've put behind bars—each of them responsible for enslaving, trafficking, exploiting, and selling dozens of children. I could also envision the corresponding hundreds and thousands of kids who wouldn't need to be rescued because their potential captors were locked up and put away.

All of this is the butterfly effect of one man who is a great father. To me, Guesno is the father of every kid we've ever rescued. Without Guesno, there would be no Operation Underground Railroad. He is the inspiration behind the liberation of some of the most precious spirits sent to this earth. Whether you're a committed father to your own children within your own home, or you're a father like Guesno, extending your arms to the fatherless, there is a butterfly effect that takes place. To be a good father is the most manly and godly thing a man can do in this life.

If I could say one thing to every father who reads this book, it would be this: pay attention. Because you have no idea how important your contribution to the rising generation will be. In the most desperate way, we need fathers like Guesno, who are striving to be like the ultimate father, our Heavenly Father, who is constantly and consistently working for our good.

In *Dads Who Stay and Fight*, Greg Trimble provides a timeless image of the attributes of fathers, like Guesno, who stay and fight in a world that needs protection from an increasing amount of evil. There is no greater cause and no greater calling than to be a dad! It's all up to you! Let's go!

GOD BLESS YOU DEAR FATHERS

INTRODUCTION

God bless you, dear fathers.
Gordon B. Hinckley[1]

IN THE SUMMER of 2016, and for the first time ever, I took my family on a vacation. I mean an actual real vacation! I hadn't taken my family on a real vacation . . . well . . . ever. I had started a business in college, and in my first eight years as a husband and father, I had been so busy running a business that it seemed impossible for me to disconnect from the many responsibilities I had. Don't get me wrong—my family and I hung out together all the time and did lots of little things together, but never something like this. This time, we packed up and got in an RV and set out to drive from coast to coast, starting on the West Coast in sunny Southern California and ending up in Washington, D. C. I feel like I did more on this trip to contribute to the desired legacy I'd like to leave as a father than at any other time in my life. I spent my time— my valuable time—on the people who deserved it and needed it the most. We wrote a song together. We sang together. We bore our testimonies to each other. We ate together. We took pictures together. We spent dedicated and undivided time together, and it was amazing.

As I was driving on Highway 90 across the South Dakota plains, everyone in the RV was doing their own thing and I was left to my own thoughts. I sat there and stared at the golden brown fields of wheat for hours on end, listening to an audiobook on business from a successful startup founder and venture capitalist. I'm constantly looking for any piece of advice that will help me become a better businessman and leader so that I can always put food on the table for my family. There are thousands of business books, self-help books, books about how to get rich, and books about how to become powerful, but as I listened to this audiobook, I wondered why I couldn't for the life of me find a book that gave me specific advice on how to become a better dad. Why is it that we equate success in our society with becoming rich and powerful when our true measure of success stares us right in the face every time we walk through our front door after a long day at work?

When I get down to defining who I want to be as a person, I want to be described in three simple ways: as a husband, a dad, and a member of The Church of Jesus Christ of Latter-day Saints. Those are three things I'm really proud of, and as far as I'm concerned, those three attributes are completely intertwined. The only thing I've ever truly hoped for in this life is that I could continue to be a dad, a husband, and a family man. The Church of Jesus Christ of Latter-day Saints is the only religion that I know of that truly describes God as a family man and promises me (as part of its doctrine) the opportunity to be a dad, a husband, and a family man in the eternities.

Because of this one doctrine alone, I've come to the logical conclusion that The Church of Jesus Christ of Latter-day Saints and its doctrine is the only logical place for me to place my bets. I want to be with my family. Plain and simple. It's not some kind of cultural conditioning. That desire to be with my family is woven into every cell of my body. I can feel that innate drive to be with them more than anything else in my life. Without that ultimate eternal possibility, life seems meaningless to me. Through all of my studies in life, I've only found one happy ending to this mortal debacle we're in—the hope that I can continue to be a dad and a husband. Anything short of that for me personally is an entirely depressing future to consider.

In this book, I'm going to focus specifically on being the kind of dad that fights against what the world is trying to do to his family. If good men don't grow up to be good dads, then the family will suffer to no end. We can't let that happen. We've got to fight. There's nothing in this world that I'm more passionate about than being a dad. It's an opportunity I have dreamed of since I was a young man. Some men dream of being rich and famous, powerful and popular, but my dream and desire has always been simple and straightforward; I've always wanted to be loved and respected by those who call me "dad." All I can ever hope for in this life is that someday my wife and kids will look back and remember me as their hero. I want to go down to my grave knowing that I did everything I could to honor the privilege and responsibility of fatherhood, and be certain that my family holds me in high esteem for my dedication and devotion to them.

It's important for us dads to focus on what's most important in life. I believe it's our responsibility to man up and fight against the evils that surround us. This book outlines some of the most important ways that we can build and maintain an impenetrable spiritual fortress for our families.

To every dad that wishes his family could grasp the emotions and love he has in his heart for them, this book is for you.

NOTES

1. Gordon B. Hinckley, "'Great Shall Be the Peace of Thy Children,'" *Ensign*, November 2000.

WHAT GOOD
DADS DO

DADS WHO STAY AND FIGHT

Rise up, O men of God!
William P. Merrill[1]

THERE WAS NEVER a time in the history of this world when good dads were needed more. Sadly, many dads are not living up to that grand opportunity and responsibility. There are too many men acting like boys and too many boys with a convoluted idea about what it means to become a man. Elder D. Todd Christofferson, borrowing some language from the Book of Mormon prophet Lehi, gave this succinct piece of advice: "We must arise from the dust of self-indulgence and be men! It is a wonderful aspiration for a boy to become a man—strong and capable; someone who can build and create things, run things; someone who makes a difference in the world."[2]

But some men that become dads are unprepared for the responsibility associated with that great title. Some dads tuck tail and run for the hills to preserve and perpetuate a life of "freedom." They leave mom and baby to fend for themselves in a brutal world while they seek a new thrill. These men still want to be boys. According to the US Census Bureau, twenty-four million children in America (one out of every three children) live in biological-father-absent homes.[3] Elder Jeffrey R. Holland was "alarmed" by this same epidemic that is sweeping the world.[4] He references a book called *Fatherless America*, wherein the author states that "fatherlessness" was "the most harmful demographic trend of this generation"[5] and the "leading cause of declining child well-being in our society."[6] Elder Holland went on to say that "Of even greater concern than the physical absenteeism of some fathers is the spiritually or emotionally absent father."[7]

A man that sees his fatherly role as a divine call will not be content to just "stick around." Instead, he will commit his entire life to making the world a better place for his family. One of my all-time favorite "dad" movies is called *Cinderella Man*. It's based on the true story of a man named Jim Braddock—a boxer who lost everything in the Great Depression. All he had left was his family and his integrity. He didn't have enough money to pay the bills, turn the heat on, run the lights, or put food on the table. Many men during this time cracked under the pressure and left their families. In the movie, there's a scene where Jim goes outside to get the milk bottles off the doorstep . . . but they are empty.

The pain of a dad who is doing his best but is unable to provide for his family elicits a "fight or flight" response. Jim Braddock, the boxer and father, had to determine whether he was going to run away from this monster of a circumstance or stay and fight!

Jim had to start from scratch to provide for his family. He borrowed some money to get the heat turned back on and get back on his feet. He worked any job he could find for piddling amounts and was lucky to find sporadic work as a dockworker. Eventually, Jim was able to claw his way out of a very bad situation and box for a living once again. In the movie, one of the reporters asked Jim Braddock what had changed in the way that he was fighting. Jim responded, "I know what I'm fighting for."

The reporter asked, "Yeah? What's that, Jimmy?"

Jim simply responded, "Milk."[8]

None of the reporters could comprehend the depth of that comment.

The real Jim Braddock said of his situation, "I'm training for a fight. Not a boxing contest or a clownin' contest or a dance. Whether it goes one round or three rounds or ten rounds, it will be a fight and a fight all the way. When you've been through what I've had to face in the last two years, a Max Baer or a Bengal tiger looks like a house pet. He might come at me with a cannon and a blackjack, and he would still be a picnic compared to what I've had to face."[9]

In *Cinderella Man*, during Jim's Art Lasky fight, Jim gets pummeled and it doesn't seem like he'll be able to last any longer. Then Lasky gives Jim his best shot, sending Jim's mouthguard flying across the ring. The screen goes white and Jim sees stars. You think he might go down for the count, but hazy images of his kids—starving, grungy, and shivering in the cold—flash across his mind. That's what Jim is fighting for. He can't go down. Not now. Not like this. His kids need him. His wife needs him. His family needs him to man up and fight. The image of his family's destitution gives him a renewed sense of fight. He picks up his mouthpiece and smiles at his opponent as if to say, "Bring it on." Jim is fighting for milk.[10]

In like manner, Jesus knew what He was fighting for when He began His journey up that lonely hill to the Garden of Gethsemane. He knew that He was walking into a war zone—by far the fiercest, most important battle this earth has ever seen. He walked into that battle for His family. Was He going to stay and fight? Or was He going to run? He knew the landscape and geography of that region very well. He knew exactly where He was situated on that ancient hill. All He had to do to avoid bleeding from every pore, enduring thirty-nine scourges with a thronged whip that ripped chunks of flesh from His back, and His impending Crucifixion was to walk up that hill over into the Judean desert.[11] He could have gone quietly, and no one would have heard from Him again. No one could have traced Him . . . but He stayed. He endured. He fought for His family.

The good dads I know would rather be beaten to a pulp than watch their families suffer. These dads don't just stick around; they fight and they fight hard. They know what they're fighting for.

NOTES

1. "Rise Up, O Men of God!," *Hymns*, 323.
2. D. Todd Christofferson, "Let Us Be Men," *Ensign*, November 2006.
3. "Father Absence + Involvement Statistics," *National Fatherhood Initiative*, January 18, 2017, www.fatherhood.org/fatherhood -data-statistics.
4. Jeffrey R. Holland, "The Hands of the Fathers," *Ensign*, May 1999.
5. David Blankenhorn, *Fatherless America: Confronting Our Most Urgent Social Problem* (New York: HarperPerennial, 1995), 1.
6. Ibid.
7. Jeffrey R. Holland, "The Hands of the Fathers," *Ensign*, May 1999.
8. *Cinderella Man*, directed by Ron Howard (Universal City, CA: Universal Studios, 2005), DVD.
9. Ellen Allbeck Maurer, *Snicklefritz: Winifred Elizabeth Manning Allbeck Tells Stories from an Earlier Time* (Minneapolis, MN: Mill City Press, 2016), 305.
10. *Cinderella Man*, directed by Ron Howard (Universal City, CA: Universal Studios, 2005), DVD.
11. *The Eternal Christ* (Novus Visum, 2010), DVD.

DADS WHO PRIORITIZE

If there were a Hall of Fame for husbands and dads, I'd make it my number one goal to get there.

Steve Young, Hall of Fame quarterback[1]

MOST DADS WORK . . . a lot! Good dads work for the security and livelihood of their families, not for the glory and recognition of the world. Business relationships come and go on a whim or a preference, but family lasts forever. These good dads go out into the world to fight for their wife and their kids because that is what's most important to them. They take their responsibility seriously because at the end of the day, their deepest desire is to be respected and loved by their wife and kids. Everyone else takes a back seat.

When you ask most of these busy working dads what their favorite part of the day is they'll likely relate similar experiences. They usually go something like this:

After dealing with the constant threat of trying to make a living, you get in your car to drive home. Sometimes your mind is racing with the events of the day. Stress is no stranger, but is a constant companion that rides with you all the way to your driveway. You sit there for a second—inhale, exhale—and muster up the strength to drag yourself out of the car. You start up the walkway toward the front door, hoping you can give your family the attention they deserve. You pray that work won't affect your countenance, and that the headache you've been working on all day will disappear. Sometimes you see little faces looking at you from the window as you approach the porch. You get to the front door and jiggle the handle. You hear footsteps that sound like a herd of cattle. Your kids unlock and swing open the door as if they've been waiting for you all day long. They swarm you, tackle you, and let out a screeching synchronous yell: "Dad!" In a single moment, all of the stress and anxiety you endured throughout the day just seems to fade away.

Above my office desk sits a framed poem with a picture of my two kids. My wife gave it to me as a present to take to my office. I have it placed on the wall right behind my desk to remind me what life is all about when making a living tries to consume me. The poem reads:

> I would rather be the daddy
> Of a romping, roguish crew,
> Of a bright-eyed chubby laddie
> And a little girl or two,
> Than the monarch of a nation
> In his high and lofty seat
> Taking empty adoration
> From the subjects at his feet.
>
> I would rather own their kisses
> As at night to me they run,
> Than to be the king who misses
> All the simpler forms of fun.
> When his dreary day is ending
> He is dismally alone,
> But when my sun is descending
> There are joys for me to own.

He may ride to horns and drumming;
I must walk a quiet street,
But when once they see me coming
Then on joyous, flying feet
They come racing to me madly
And I catch them with a swing
And I say it proudly, gladly,
That I'm happier than a king.

You may talk of lofty places,
You may boast of pomp and power,
Men may turn their eager faces
To the glory of an hour,
But give me the humble station
With its joys that long survive,
For the daddies of the nation
Are the happiest men alive.[2]

To be effective dads and husbands, we need to try to worry less about what the world thinks. We may strive to impress people who we *think* are important, while neglecting the people who we *know* are most important. Why do we do this? Even if we're able to impress a few people, or maybe even a lot of people, we will certainly never be able to impress everyone, and the people in the world we do manage to impress will forget about us in an instant. Sadly, the world has a "what have you done for me lately" mentality. The minute someone perceives that you are no longer of value to them, they'll drop you flat on your face. But those little ones who run to you with joy and gladness will hold you up forever . . . as long as they are first on your priority list.

Many people know the name Steve Young. He was a BYU stud of a quarterback, a San Francisco 49ers hometown hero, and an eventual NFL football Hall of Fame inductee. He was agile, tough, and persistent in everything that he did. But few people know the name Grit Young. Grit was a nickname for LeGrande Young, Steve Young's dad. Steve Young attributes much of his success on and off the football field to his dad. In an interview, Grit talked about spending time with his kids. "I was with them a lot," Grit said, "and tried to be with them, and that's the way you show love in my opinion."[3] That's really what it takes—our time. Prioritizing our family over the things that might distract us from being a dad.

As this all-time great quarterback, Steve Young, concluded his induction speech into the Hall of Fame, he said maybe the most important words of his entire professional career, "I sincerely love my family and know that being a Hall of Fame husband and dad is what will eventually define my life."[4] After everything Steve had been through, and after all he had accomplished, he knew that everything else pales in comparison to the responsibility and opportunity of being a dad.

NOTES

1. Steve Young in Tom Limbert, *Dad's Playbook: Wisdom for Fathers from the Greatest Coaches of All Time* (San Francisco: Chronicle Books LLC, 2012), 9.
2. Edgar A. Guest, "Daddies."
3. *Grit: The True Story of Steve Young* (Cedar Fort, 2015), DVD; see also "Grit The True Story of Steve Young," YouTube video, 4:21, posted by Katherine Thornburgh, May 13, 2015, www .youtube.com/watch?v=UYBVSqb2qCw.
4. Steve Young in Tom Limbert, *Dad's Playbook: Wisdom for Fathers from the Greatest Coaches of All Time* (San Francisco: Chronicle Books LLC, 2012), 9.

DADS UNDERNEATH THE STARS

You have succeeded in life when all you really want is only what you really need.
Vernon Howard[1]

DO YOU REMEMBER stressing over finding the perfect Christmas gifts for your kids only to have them open all of their presents and fall in love with the little toy you got at the dollar store? You probably thought to yourself, "I could have saved five hundred bucks and only spent a dollar at the dollar store and the kid would have been just as happy." Well, that all-too-common circumstance is a microcosm of one of the grand truths of raising kids and being a good dad.

If you're like me, you spend a great deal of your life trying to figure out how to provide a good life for your kids. You constantly think about and worry about whether you are coming up short as a parent. You worry that somehow your inability to create an ideal situation for your kids will taint their childhood and ruin their life, and it will be all your fault. You worry about the time going by so fast and about not creating enough memories with your kids.

Many times we link all of our shortcomings back to money. We think to ourselves, "If I made a little more money, I could do so much more for my kids." Unfortunately, for most young parents, a lot of money is not an option. But is that really such a bad thing?

17

Lindsey Stirling, one of the greatest violinists of our day, said,

> Through my entire childhood, my family struggled financially, however I would not trade my humble childhood years for anything else. It was during these years that I learned that a pair of scissors and a bottle of paint could transform a refrigerator boxes [sic] into a spaceship adventure to mars, that a tattered pink dress once put on could become a ball gown, and that eating a bowl of cereal on the living room floor with my dad was quality time. In spite of the many limitations that could have boxed me in, it was these years that taught me to dream big, work hard and enjoy the small simple moments of life.[2]

Think about the following hypothetical scenario for a second. You just won the lottery. You now have as much money as you'd ever need to "do so much more for your kids." What would you do? Would you vacation 24/7? Never work again? Buy your kids designer clothes? Get them an endless supply of toys? You could do anything you wanted! Life would be a breeze, and the kids would be "set for life!" Right?

But then a few months go by and you start to realize that none of those things were ever the best things for your kids. You realize that your kids aren't "better off" or happier. In fact, now they start to expect everything. You don't need to experience a sudden influx of cash to know that this is true. Just study the lives of the kids of the rich and famous. So many of them have no idea how to function in society. They have no idea how to take care of themselves or work hard. Regardless of how much money you have and how many "experiences" you've had with your kids, they've forgotten them all. Now all they wish for is self-sufficiency. But they've never seen that side of life and have no idea where to start.

When I was growing up, my family was close to being considered poor. My dad didn't start making good money until after I was eighteen. I watched him bootstrap his own company with no help from anyone. My mom and I cruised around in a beat-up Monte Carlo that used to backfire down the road. We were lucky to have a car. We rented modest little homes. I remember working hard every weekend with my dad shoveling dirt, mowing lawns, pulling weeds, and riding in trailers to the local dump. If I earned five bucks, I was rich. I learned how to pitch in and how to work hard. At that age, I never could have imagined how it would impact my work ethic down the road.

My parents probably wished every day of their life that they could do more for me. But if we had been rich, I probably wouldn't have had those experiences working with my dad in the yard. I wouldn't have learned to be grateful when my mom bought me a couple shirts at Mervyn's for back to school. Those experiences . . . I remember. For some reason, I remember.

Elder Dallin H. Oaks once shared how a friend of his "took his young family on a series of summer vacation trips, including visits to memorable historic sites. At the end of the summer he asked his teenage son which of these good summer activities he enjoyed most. The father learned from the reply, and so did those he told of it. 'The thing I liked best this summer,' the boy replied, 'was the night you and I laid on the lawn and looked at the stars and talked.'"[3]

Simple. Cost effective. Memorable.

Your kids don't care how much money you make! They only care if you care. If you emphasize all of the things you wish you had, then they'll do the same and turn into covetous, insatiable adults. They'll never be able to enjoy anything because nothing will be good enough for them. When they're young and impressionable, they don't care about the things you stew and fret and worry about. All they worry about is spending time with you: time on the floor eating a bowl of cereal or lying on some scratchy grass and looking at the stars. It always seems to be those moments that last. As if it's some sort of cosmic rule that the simple things in life are the most memorable.

Your time. Your heart. Your love.

Our kids don't need more luxurious lifestyles, exotic vacations, or for us to make life easy for them. If anything, we should be making it challenging for them. Think about a sensei or karate master who takes on a protégé. Will it do the pupil any good if the master is easy on the student? No way, right? When that student gets into the real world, they are going to get their teeth kicked in. It's the master's duty and responsibility to prepare their pupil for the real world. They have a controlled environment in which the master can intelligently take the pupil to the brink of mental and physical exhaustion in order to create growth in that individual.

This sort of training makes the vicissitudes of life seem easy when the sensei is long gone. Too many of us have our thinking caps on backwards. We live our lives to make our kids' lives easier. But as we make our kids' lives easier, we also make our kids' lives harder. We get frustrated when we aren't able to give little Johnny his dream birthday or little Suzie her coveted pony. Sometimes we spend our days depressed, thinking about all of the things we don't have. We let precious time slip through our hands because of a preoccupation with what others appear to have or what we think we should have.

If you can teach your kids anything while they're young, teach them to be happy with less. If "necessity is the mother of invention,"[4] then it makes sense for us to stick with the necessities and let our kids come up with the rest. Let them be creative with what they have, instead of purchasing the creativity for them. Let them turn nothing into something. Not something into nothing. Then, if riches come their way down the road, they'll use those riches for good instead of squandering them.

NOTES

1. Jean Maalour, *Change Your World* (2013), 197.
2. "Hi I'm Lindsey Stirling," Lindsey Stirling, *Mormon.org*, January 18, 2017, www.mormon.org/me/b1nv.
3. Dallin H. Oaks, "Good, Better, Best," *Ensign*, November 2007.
4. English proverb.

DADS WHO KNOW HOW TO INVEST

*Fatherhood is not a matter
of station or wealth.*
Ezra Taft Benson[1]

IN ORDER TO be a good dad, you've got to be a good investor. But if you're picturing one of those power brokers in blue suits on the New York Stock Exchange, then I've got some explaining to do. Good dads come from various backgrounds, and while they may know very little about making money, each of them lives by a stringent set of guidelines when it comes to investing their time. Their time-investment strategies are similar to some of the most effective investment strategies that have been passed down from generation to generation as far back as the early American settlers.

The early Americans came here with little, and worked very hard for what they had. Their goal was to increase their capital in order to build an inheritance they could leave to future generations. According to President Henry B. Eyring, a former Stanford business professor, the "early Yankee families in America" taught their posterity some important rules about how to treat their inheritance. He said, "They were always to invest the capital they inherited and to live only on part of the earnings." They all seemed to have one hard-and-fast rule: "Never spend your capital."[2] They followed that rule in an effort to bless those that would follow after them. It was all about their kids, grandkids, and great-grandkids. If one of the family members spent their inheritance, it would bankrupt the entire family and leave future generations with no more capital to invest. If each family held true to the family rule of investing, the earnings on the investment of that capital would increase over time, thus enabling the capital to work for the kids, rather than the kids needing to work for the capital. In turn, their capital increase could be invested further as they lived frugally on "only . . . part of the earnings" as their predecessors did, thereby freeing them up to serve in various ways that were not possible without that precious inheritance.[3]

Many of us are not in the same financial circumstances that the American settlers were in. Even the poorest among us have much more than they had upon their arrival in this country. In fact, we seem to be in the opposite position as those early Americans. We seem to have more capital but much less time for each other. In 1877, Brigham Young, one of the brightest economic minds on the frontier, talked about our true capital and inheritance, and then laid out instructions on how to properly invest it. He said, "With regard to our property, as I have told you many times, the property which we inherit from our Heavenly Father is our time, and the power to choose in the disposition of the same. This is the real capital that is bequeathed unto us by our Heavenly Father; all the rest is what he may be pleased to add unto us."[4]

According to Brigham Young, our time is our capital, and that capital is an inheritance from God. We are given the ability and freedom to either spend our inheritance away and have nothing to show for it, or to invest our inheritance and see our capital yield future dividends. PGA golf professional Keith Clearwater once said, "If I wrestle with my kids, on the ground, in the grass, for three straight hours when I had all kinds of stuff to do, there couldn't have been a better use of my time."⁵ Sure, there were many other things that Keith could have been doing with his time, but that time with his kids was the best investment he could have made with his capital. We are being pulled in so many directions with our time. It feels as if the adversary's number-one strategy in these last days is to get dads to waste their time, instead of investing it in the things of eternal significance.

Not too long ago, I headed down to meet a very successful friend of mine at Trestles Beach in California for some sushi and a surf session. My friend Jeff has worked with some of the largest and most successful companies this world has ever seen. Jeff is now getting to the age where his kids are either on a mission, married, or about to leave on a mission. He was lamenting "life without his boys," but then went on to explain that his boys seemed closer to him now than ever before. The conversation moved on, and I didn't get a chance to ask him what he meant by that. But, after I left, I kept thinking about Jeff's declaration of being closer than ever to his kids (which seemed strange because many parents and children seem to drift apart during those teenage years). So I emailed Jeff and asked him to expound upon his relationship with his kids. Jeff replied to me and explained that a child's relationship with their dad can flourish and improve over time if "you put in the time week after week, year after year . . . always putting them first and making them your top priority." He compared this process to the "deep watering of a tree."⁶ It takes time, care, and consistency to ensure those roots are being nourished and nurtured.

From a financial perspective, wise investors have always understood the basic principle of making deposits. They know that as you invest your capital (making consistent deposits at the bank), you will eventually be able to make withdrawals. No dad can expect to make withdrawals, or any kind of return on his time investment, if he has not made a sufficient amount of deposits. It's just a basic fact of investing. If we don't invest our most precious capital—our time—into the relationships we have with our kids, then we can never expect them to take us seriously in the future. As our children get older and we ask them to sit down and have a serious conversation with us, a child is much more likely to respond, listen, and learn from that conversation if they know that we have been there for them in the past and have invested in their lives. To try and have rapport with a child after making very few deposits of our time sets us up for rejection. Their message back to us could be similar to the dreaded "insufficient funds" message at the ATM.

The Book of Mormon as we have it today is another demonstration of the dedicated and consistent investment of time from dads on behalf of their kids. From the first to the last page, the Book of Mormon can be summarized as a bunch of faithful Christian dads who wrote down their thoughts, revelations, and pieces of advice in order to help their kids. Yes, they were commanded to write those things to come forth in the latter days, but I would suspect that their greatest tangible motivation was the kids they raised and desired to teach. We often quote Moroni as the primary reason for the existence of the Book of Mormon: "Behold, I speak unto you as if ye were present, and yet ye are not. But behold, Jesus Christ hath shown you unto me, and I know your doing" (Mormon 8:35). We think, because of that verse, that the entire Book of Mormon was only written for us in our day when in reality, the children of these Book of Mormon prophets were an integral part of their motivation to keep writing. I imagine that the faces and futures of their children and grandchildren drove them to continue the monumental effort of digging and carving into those plates of ore. We do these things, says Nephi, "that our children may know to what source they may look for a remission of their sins" (2 Nephi 25:26). That is what drove those men to invest their time—the love of their children and their desire to invest the capital that was given to them as an inheritance from God.

If you ask the reputable Harvard business professor Elder Clayton M. Christensen what he considers to be one of his best investments, he might point you to an investment he made in a real estate development project long ago. Of all his investments, he would likely tell you that this one has brought him the most significant return on investment. I would venture to guess that from a financial perspective, this was also one of his least expensive investments. This investment took place shortly after the purchase of his first house. As his family settled into this new house, he saw the perfect place in their new backyard for a playhouse. He and his kids, Ann and Mathew, spent weeks working through the details of acquiring materials and ultimately building the playhouse. They put their hearts and souls into that playhouse, and since it was built from scratch, they also invested a great deal of time.[7]

Elder Christensen noted that while the house was being built, it was all the kids wanted to do. The minute he got home, they were hankering to get back to work on the project. Elder Christensen cited Herzberg's theory of motivation as the primary reason that his kids were so excited about building their playhouse, explaining that the pride they took in their own accomplishment lit the fire in them to work incessantly on the house. I'm sure that his observation is true, but I have another theory. I believe that Ann and Mathew, above all else, loved spending time with their dad, showing off for their dad, and seeing the emotions on his face as he swelled with pride in their accomplishments.[8]

As Elder Christensen looked back on the experience of building the playhouse with his kids, he said, "I shudder to think that I almost bought a kit from which I could have quickly assembled the playhouse myself."[9] Elder Christensen made a low-risk, high-reward kind of investment.

Good dads are masters at investing their time. They never spend it. They always invest it.

NOTES

1. Ezra Taft Benson, "Great Things Required of Their Fathers," *Ensign*, May 1981.
2. Henry B. Eyring, "Child of Promise," *New Era*, August 1993.
3. Ibid.
4. Brigham Young, *Journal of Discourses*, 18:354
5. Keith Clearwater in "HomeSports: Leave a Legacy," YouTube video, 4:14, posted by "HomeSports," December 20, 2013, www.youtube.com/watch?v=caYjt7OsjPs.
6. Jeff Adcock, personal correspondence with author.
7. Clayton M. Christensen, James Allworth, and Karen Dillon, *How Will You Measure Your Life?* (New York: HarperCollins, 2012), 37–38.
8. Ibid.
9. Ibid., 38.

DADS WHO DISCIPLINE

*The man who complains about
the way the ball bounces is likely
the one who dropped it.*
Lou Holtz[1]

ON OUR JOURNEY across the United States as a family, we stopped at almost every major Church history site. The nostalgia still hasn't worn off for me. But the low point of our trip was definitely when we were in Kirtland, Ohio, at the Newel K. Whitney store. Many people are unaware of how sacred this store was. The amount of faith Newel K. Whitney exercised here is extraordinary. He prayed for a prophet; Joseph Smith showed up at his store with almost nothing but his family and called Newel by name. Newel practically gave Joseph the entire store as the new Church headquarters. He gave him the office for church business; the bedroom for Emma, Joseph, and their child; the kitchen for making food; and an extra room for the School of the Prophets. Needless to say, there were a lot of important events that took place in that store, and we were standing in the same rooms where these important events happened.

My dad, my wife, my kids, and I took a tour (given by a couple of sister missionaries) through the Newel K. Whitney store. During the tour we were required to be part of a small group of other families. In this group, there was a young man who was irreverent, disruptive, disrespectful, and immature. He looked to be between fourteen and sixteen years old. As we stood there in this place, with these sister missionaries trying their hardest to create an experience for us in which the Spirit might dwell, this boy was out of control. He was drumming on all of the antiques in the store, talking loudly over the sister missionaries, and just trying to get attention. My dad and I looked at each other in awe. My dad leaned over to me and said, "Never in my life have I seen anything like this." We couldn't for the life of us figure out how this boy thought it would be all right to act like this—until the boy's dad walked into the room. And immediately, we got it. The dad started acting the same way, disrespecting the sisters (but in a more adult, laid-back sort of way). There was no discipline in the boy because there was no discipline in the father. If only Elder Larry M. Gibson had been there in that store to remind this father that "Every day you are teaching your children what it means to be a father. You are laying a foundation for the next generation."[2]

If there is one thing I've learned, it's that we are a society of finger-pointing and excuse-making human beings. We can make excuses for just about anything. Dads are bewildered and shocked when their kids don't turn out the way they think they should. But rarely do they consider that they might have neglected to discipline and teach their kids properly when they were young. If we don't train them, teach them, and discipline them while they're young, then we're going to have a much harder time trying to correct their bad habits and behaviors when they get into their teenage years. Joseph Smith said, "If we start right, it is easy to go right all the time; but if we start wrong, we may go wrong, and it will be a hard matter to get right."[3] The lack of discipline in the fathers results in a lack of discipline in their children.

I heard a story once about a few kids acting up on an airplane while the parents sat there and did nothing. After this behavior went on for a while, the man on the plane who was being affected by the kids' behavior (chair getting kicked, stuff getting thrown, and so on) turned to the dad and politely asked him if he could get control of his kids. The father of the kids responded to this man by telling him to relax and that he was "just letting kids be kids." All of us have seen this attitude before. "Letting kids be kids" is a lame excuse for being an oblivious parent. Sure, there are times when it's appropriate for us to allow our kids to run wild and crazy, but never should it disrespect another person. Helping our children recognize that there's a time and place for everything will be key to their future success as people.

We can discipline and parent a child without ruining their childhood. In fact, failing to discipline a child properly might ruin their childhood and adulthood for good. It's our job to train our kids to be responsible and respectful adults, and there is no better time to do that than when your kids look up to you the most. If kids become accustomed to acting however they want without any consequences, then they will act that way as teenagers. By the time you try and correct that behavior, it's too late; now they've locked onto their independence and tend to rebel. Now you have a kid who hasn't learned how to act and who is finding their own independence. That's a scary combination. But train them while they're young, and you won't need to discipline them when they're older because they will have learned self-discipline. Learning the correct balance of discipline and correction will actually improve your relationship with your kids in the long term. They will respect you and be grateful that they've learned how to function correctly in society.

Los Angeles Dodgers head coach Tommy Lasorda said, "Managing is like holding a dove in your hand. Squeeze too hard and you kill it, not hard enough and it flies away."[4] UCLA basketball coach John Wooden said that we should "be slow to criticize and quick to commend."[5] Our great Redeemer Jesus Christ says that we should be "reproving . . . with sharpness," but then should always display afterwards "an increase of love toward him whom thou hast reproved, lest he esteem thee to be his enemy" (D&C 121:43). There is an art to discipline. It can be done in a way that lets your kids love and respect you. Or it can be done in a way that pushes a child away for good and causes rebellion. It can be calculated to lift and to bless, or it can be used recklessly to belittle and destroy. But one thing is certain; a dad that learns how to properly discipline his kids will glory in their character for the rest of his days.

NOTES

1. Lou Holtz in Tom Limbert, *Dad's Playbook: Wisdom for Fathers from the Greatest Coaches of All Time* (San Francisco: Chronicle Books, 2012), 114.

2. Larry M. Gibson, "Fatherhood—Our Eternal Destiny," *Ensign*, May 2015.

3. "History, 1838–1856, volume E–1 [1 July 1843–30 April 1844]," *The Joseph Smith Papers*, accessed January 20, 2017, 1968; www .josephsmithpapers.org/paper-summary/history-1838-1856 -volume-e-1-1-july-1843-30-april-1844/340?highlight=if%20 we%20start%20right%2C%20it%20is%20easy%20to%20 go%20right%20all%20the%20time.

4. Tommy Lasorda in Tom Limbert, *Dad's Playbook: Wisdom for Fathers from the Greatest Coaches of All Time* (San Francisco: Chronicle Books, 2012), 25.

5. John Wooden in Tom Limbert, *Dad's Playbook: Wisdom for Fathers from the Greatest Coaches of All Time* (San Francisco: Chronicle Books, 2012), 44.

DADS WHO
TEACH THEIR
KIDS TO WORK

My Father worketh hitherto, and I work.
Jesus Christ[1]

MY WIFE KRISTYN and I were flying back from Boston to Los Angeles after I had finished speaking at a social media conference for some stakes in the Cambridge area. She was in the process of proofreading this very book on the airplane when she leaned over to me and asked a really important question.

"Greg," she asked, "Do you have a table of contents?"

"Sure," I said, "But why do you ask?"

"Because you've done a really good job at emphasizing the need for a dad to focus on his family and not get too caught up in the things of the world, but I think one of the most important things a dad can teach his kids is how to work hard. I haven't seen a chapter on the value of work ethic yet, and I would hate for people to get the wrong idea from what you've written so far that a dad can be justified in shirking his work responsibilities to just 'have fun with the family' all of the time."

She continued, "You need to write one more chapter on the value of hard work!" I agreed immediately, and then remembered a blog post that she had written previously that was entitled "5 Ways

You Know You've Found the 'Right Man'."[2] In this post, she addressed other women who were in the process of choosing a husband. She explained why a woman should gravitate toward a man who knows the value of hard work. She began by stating,

> It is very difficult . . . even near impossible for a woman to respect her husband if he is lazy and doesn't try his hardest to provide for his family. That being said . . . there is a big difference between not making a lot of money and being lazy! A woman can greatly respect her man who works hard everyday for his family but because of circumstances, is not able to make a ton of money. A woman can also have full respect and admiration for her husband if he is unemployed because of circumstances beyond his control . . . especially in this economy right now . . . as long as he is working his hardest to become employed again. What a woman can't respect however, (call it a woman's survival instinct for her offspring or what have you) is a man who puts his pleasure above working hard for the family. Whether he is just plain lazy and doesn't feel like working or he would rather be watching T.V. or playing video or computer games, this plants a seed of resentment into the heart of the woman that is hard to overcome.[3]

Kids, especially little boys, are going to gravitate toward the things their dads are interested in. If a dad is into creating things, building things, and progressing in life, then it is likely that his kids will also follow that path. If the kids only see their dad consuming the creations and services of others, then those kids will probably become great consumers instead of great creators. If the dad is consistently choosing the easy route, then the children will generally choose likewise. Watching a dad do hard things in life, struggle through challenging times, and persist through trials will be some of the most important observations a child can have early in their life. These observations will give the child strength when they face their mountains in life.

Dave Ramsey said it this way:

> You should view teaching your children to work in the same way you view teaching them to bathe and brush their teeth—as a necessary skill for life. An adult who has no clue how to tackle a job and finish it with vigor is as debilitated as an adult with green teeth and body odor. If your child graduates from high school and his only skill set consists of playing video games, whining, copping an attitude of entitlement, and eating junk food, you have set him up to fail.[4]

Our kids may not want to hear that they need to go out and pull weeds or complete a set of recurring chores before they can do anything else, but that is exactly what they need. A dad who is proactively engaged in improving himself will see those same attributes take root in his children. This concept is what caused my wife to encourage her unmarried girlfriends to

> Find a man that is developing a skill. He's not a time waster and understands the urgency behind providing a decent living for the family in a competitive world. Get into his past so you can identify his previous accomplishments. Look for things that have required perseverance and determination so that you know he won't quit on you at the first sign of resistance. No woman wants a momma's boy that is always looking for the next handout.[5]

Women want a man who is tough and willing to get out there and get things done. They want a man whom they feel secure around. They want to be able to look at that man and know in their heart that everything will be okay. Regardless of the circumstances, women want to know that he will be there for them and for their kids; that he'll do what it takes to look after them, and that he'll use every last ounce of strength he has to get it done. These moms don't look to their husbands in this way because they're helpless or incapable of taking care of themselves. They look to their husbands to display these attributes so that her children will gain the vital attributes of success and happiness. A mother wants her children to know what a real man is. For her son, she wants a role model and a hero. For her daughter, she dreams of a worthy son-in-law chosen based on the solid attributes of the father her daughter observed.

All of this, all of the goodness, all of the blessings in life, in faith, in relationships, and in eternity revolve around the concept of hard work. Each marriage. Each career. Each calling. Each challenge. Each trial. Everything that we are and everything that we have the potential to become centers around our ability and capacity to endure hard work. The persistence and tenacity of the fathers will be the seeds of success planted in the children.

NOTES

1. John 5:17.
2. Kristyn Trimble, "5 Ways You Know You've Found the 'Right Man'," *GregTrimble.com*, www.gregtrimble.com/5-ways-you -know-youve-found-the-right-man.
3. Ibid.
4. "Why Kids Need to Experience the Value of Hard Work," *Dave Ramsey*, January 20, 2017, www.daveramsey.com/blog /why-kids-need-value-hard-work.

5. Kristyn Trimble, "5 Ways You Know You've Found the 'Right Man'," *GregTrimble.com*, www.gregtrimble.com/5-ways-you-know-youve-found-the-right-man.

DADS WHO TEACH

You cannot teach a man anything; you can only help him find it within himself.

Galileo[1]

THERE ARE MANY dads who try to teach their kids at every opportunity they can get. Unfortunately, many times the kids aren't listening because of the way the message is being delivered. "You can lead a horse to water, but you can't make him drink" is only partially true. There's actually a lot you can do to help him drink. What you need to do is "salt the oats" that you're feeding him. If you lead a thirsty horse to water, there's a much greater chance that this horse will go ahead and drink. Likewise, you can make your kids thirsty for the things you're teaching by "salting the oats." The Apostle Paul told the Colossians to "Let your speech be alway with grace, seasoned with salt, that ye may know how ye ought to answer every man" (Colossians 4:6). When teaching your kids about life, make sure to add salt!

My mission president was a great teacher. I always looked forward to mission conferences so that I could listen to him speak. I asked him one day, "What's the secret to teaching like that?"

I knew that the most important things to do were to have the Spirit and to know the doctrine. But there were many people that had the Spirit and knew the doctrine that never had the power to motivate the people they were teaching. So what was it? What was his secret?

"Elder, you've got to become a great storyteller," he said.

What? That's it?

But as I thought about his counsel and implemented it in my teaching, I could immediately see the difference. Stories are interesting. Everyone has a story, and the better you tell that story, the more people will be able to identify with you. You've got to make them feel like they were there in order for them to grasp the spirit of the occasion. Whether it's your story or the story of the scriptures, you've got to immerse your kids in it, and the only way for you to immerse them in it is to immerse yourself in it first. When I asked my friend Ken Krogue (founder of the multi-billion-dollar, Provo-based company Inside Sales) what he wished he knew as a young dad, he responded, "Become good at telling stories that touch the heart and the mind with truth."[2]

Elder M. Russell Ballard once said, "Water cannot be drawn from an empty well."[3] The same goes for your ability to teach, express, and expound upon the stories that are found in the scriptures and in life's frequent lessons. You've got to put water in your well if you'd like to draw from it at a later date. It's not enough to just recite clichés all day.

When teaching your kids, the delivery is everything. They don't want to hear you preach. They don't want a lecture or a sermon. Instead of telling them that you're going to *teach* them something and then ascending your Rameumptom to do so, ask them if you can *share* with them a story that relates to the thing you'd like to teach them. This will keep their brains active and alert, instead of shutting down because "Dad's in sermonizing mode again." You can't actually become a teacher to your child until they invite you into their heart as their teacher. The gospel and other character-building principles have been likened to a sweet piece of fruit. You are the one carrying and delivering that fruit. The way in which you present and deliver the fruit could make or break whether someone allows you to feed it to them. No one likes to eat food that is presented poorly, regardless of how good someone says it tastes.

There's a trust factor built into their taste buds. If what you're trying to present to your kids tastes sweet to you, then make sure you present it neatly and carefully in order to ensure that you don't turn them off before they ever have a chance to taste it for themselves.

Good teachers are good presenters. Many people possess great knowledge and marvelous experiences, but are never able to get those things into the hearts and minds of others because of their presentation abilities. Present well, and your kids will listen to every word you say.

NOTES

1. Jeffrey Bennett, "Galileo put us in our place," *Los Angeles Times*, February 8, 2009.
2. Ken Krogue, personal correspondence with author.
3. M. Russell Ballard, "Daughters of God," *Ensign*, May 2008.

QUALITIES OF GOOD DADS

DADS WHO LOVE HARD

Could we with ink the ocean fill, and were the
skies of parchment made; / Were every stalk
on earth a quill, And every man a scribe by
trade: / To write the love of God above would
drain the ocean dry, / Nor could the scroll contain
the whole though stretched from sky to sky.
The Love of God[1]

THE PURPOSE OF this life is to learn how to love. The oft
quoted "God is love" (1 John 4:8) is actually pretty darn accurate
when you think about it. For us to become like God, we have to
learn to love the way God loves. Much of the world doesn't comprehend true love. That word "love" gets thrown around without
much real meaning behind it. But what is true love? What is real,
lasting, enduring love?

The purest form of love ever exhibited on this earth took place
as Christ entered the Garden of Gethsemane. Both the Father and
the Son showed us what love truly is. Heavenly Father had to sit
there and watch as His innocent Son was tortured and desecrated.
Can you imagine such a scene? To have the power to do something
about it, and yet remain still? "I am a father," Elder Holland once
stated, "but I cannot comprehend the burden it must have been for
God in His heaven to witness the deep suffering and Crucifixion
of His Beloved Son in such a manner. His every impulse and
instinct *must* have been to stop it, . . . but He did not intervene."[2]

As a dad myself, I can't imagine how painful that must have been for Him.

I've always wondered how Christ was able to go through with the Atonement. How was it that He was able to endure the type of pain He had to endure for people that He had never even met in the flesh? What kind of love would have to exist in one person's heart to drive them to take on such a task? I learned the answer to that question on the night of my first child's birth.

My daughter, Taylor, was born during Passover time in April of 2006. The delivery wasn't going as planned. Her heart would beat horribly fast and then painfully slow. The doctors determined that the umbilical cord was wrapped around her neck and was choking her out. My wife was in all kinds of pain. We had been up for over thirty-six hours and I was standing there helpless. There was absolutely nothing I could do for these two people I loved so much.

Amidst the hospital chaos, time seemed to stand still, and for the first time in my life I truly comprehended the love of God. I stood there, leaning over the hospital bed next to my wife, not knowing why I was visualizing the Garden of Gethsemane at the height of this emotional roller coaster, but it was all I could see with my mind's eyes. She was writhing in pain, the baby heart monitor was jumping back and forth, and the doctors and nurses were frantically trying to figure out what to do. I looked down at my wife in pain and all I could think of was that I would do anything to take her place. I truly wanted to take her pain. If she was going to die, I wanted to die for her. If my daughter was going to suffocate from a wrapped umbilical cord, I wanted to take her place and suffocate for her.

My mind flashed back to Gethsemane (which in the Hebrew means "olive-press")³ and I visualized the Savior being "pressed"—enduring immense physical and spiritual torment.

I looked back at my wife.

John 15:13 came to my mind: "Greater love hath no man than this, that a man lay down his life for his friends."

Then 1 John 3:16 came next: "Hereby perceive we the love of God, because he laid down his life for us: and we ought to lay down our lives."

In that moment, it was as if I could feel what drove Christ to complete His mission. I could feel the true love that was within Him and it was the most powerful emotion I had ever felt. Because of the love I felt for my wife and daughter, I would have done anything—even to the enduring of a long and torturous death, if necessary—in order to save them. I would fight tooth and nail until my last breath to make sure they lived on. And that, I realized, is exactly what Christ did for us in the Garden and on the Cross. If I was given the choice, nothing could have stopped me from taking their place. The love I felt for them, I believe was the love that Christ felt for us—His family members—as He took our pains, afflictions, and ultimate death upon Himself. The very thought of my family suffering stirred a love within me that can only be described as divine.

Because Christ knew all of us before we came to earth, He was able to draw upon the memories and the love He had for each and every one of us. The thought of our suffering motivated Him to go through with it. He didn't want to do it. In fact, He asked for that "bitter cup" (D&C 19:18) to be removed from Him if there was any other way, but His familial, even fatherly, love is what enabled Him to endure and fight until he had overcome.

NOTES

1. Frederick M. Lehman, *The Love of God* (1917).
2. Jeffrey R. Holland, "The Hands of the Fathers," *Ensign*, May 1999; italics in original.
3. Guide to the Scriptures, "Gethsemane"; scriptures.lds.org.

DADS WITH SOFT HEARTS

I was eyes to the blind,
and feet was I to the lame.
I was a father to the poor:
and the cause which I knew
not I searched out.

Job[1]

ON SATURDAY, OCTOBER 11, 1986, Roger "The Rocket" Clemens took the mound at Angel stadium as the starting pitcher for the Boston Red Sox as they faced off against the Anaheim Angels in game four of the American League Championship Series (ALCS). Clemens threw seven innings of shutout baseball and was eventually yanked by his manager in the ninth inning because of a lead-off homer and a pair of base hits. The Boston manager John McNamara brought in relief pitcher Calvin Schiraldi who led the Boston pitching staff with a 1.41 ERA.[2] Schiraldi eventually gave up a couple runs and the game was tied at 3-3.[3]

This game's outcome didn't mean much to me. I was only six years old when it took place. But what happened at that game all these years later means the world to me. You see, my dad was there at that game, a semi-recent convert who was lucky enough to get playoff tickets with some friends from his ward.

This game and this series in 1986 between the Angels and the Red Sox was thought by some to be one of the best playoff series in baseball history. As game four went into extra innings and that stadium was rockin', my dad decided to head downstairs to grab some food before the top of the tenth inning. Because it was so late in the game, he was alone in the hallways with virtually no one else looking for food. But, as he was walking, he saw a man he recognized: Ted Williams, one of the best all-time hitters in baseball and one of my dad's heroes. His loyalty to the Red Sox for nineteen seasons, his service in both World War II and the Korean War, his seventeen All-Star appearances, and his baseball records made Williams a hero to almost all baseball fans of his time.[4] You don't meet Ted Williams in the halls coincidentally all that often, especially since he had been retired for some time at that point. This was a big deal. My dad didn't have anything for him to sign so he just asked to shake his hand. At that moment, a kid ran up with a program and asked Ted to sign the program. My dad asked the kid to rip off part of his program so that he could get his signature as well. My dad, elated, headed back to his friends in left field with no food, but with a Ted Williams signature in his hand.

Throughout the game, my dad and his friends had been going back and forth with a few Boston fans that were sitting behind them. It was all in good fun. One particular dad who had brought his son who was partially disabled to the game was hassling my dad and his friends all game. These were die-hard Boston fans—and if you've been to an Angels and Red Sox game, then you know how tense that can get. But when my dad showed up with Ted Williams's signature, that dad and his son lost their minds. Jealousy didn't even begin to describe the scene. All of this was taking place while the Angels were rallying for the win in the bottom of the eleventh inning. The Angels pulled off an amazing comeback, leaving Red Sox fans—including the father and son behind my dad—stunned in their seats. When the game was over, my dad, knowing how much this boy loved Ted Williams, turned around and offered the signed program to the boy. The dad, flattered and shocked, declined based on the value of the signature.

"We can't take that," he said.

"Please, take it for your son," my dad insisted.

After some back and forth, the boy finally took the Ted Williams signature. My dad said that when this boy set his finger on that signature, his face lit up with pure excitement and joy. My dad was in possession of that once-in-a-lifetime sentimental signature for only two intense innings of a baseball game. And then it was gone, given to someone he felt a great deal of love and compassion for.

In my mind, I will always have the image of my dad handing his Ted Williams autograph to that boy. I will forever have the image of that boy's face lighting up because of my dad. In that situation, and in countless others I witnessed, my dad, in effect, "took the shirt off his back" and gave it to someone less fortunate. Seeing this quality in my dad solidified my desire to always look for someone to lift up and bless.

A dad with a soft heart isn't soft, just as much as a meek man isn't weak. The dads with hard hearts are the ones we need to worry about. They are the ones who will tuck tail and run in order to save their own skin. They don't feel for others and are thereby unable to draw upon strong emotions of love to carry them through a fight. In contrast, dads with soft hearts are usually tough as nails, and their powerful emotions and desire to protect turns them into warriors.

NOTES

1. Job 29:15–16.
2. "Calvin Schiraldi," *Baseball-Reference.com*, February 18,2017, www.baseball-reference.com/players/s/schirca01.shtml.

3. "Oct. 11, 1986, Red Sox at Angels Box Score and Play by Play," *Baseball-Reference.com*, February 18, 2017, http://www .baseball-reference.com/boxes/CAL/CAL198610110.shtml.

4. "Ted Williams," *National Baseball Hall of Fame*, February 18, 2017, http://baseballhall.org/hof/williams-ted; "Ted Williams," *Baseball-Reference.com*, February 18, 2017, www .baseball-reference.com/players/w/willite01.shtml.

DADS WHO LISTEN

Wisdom will come as we listen to learn.
Russell M. Nelson[1]

ONE OF THE most neglected skills to master as a father is the skill of listening. Hey, just ask your wife. I'm sure she'll agree. President Henry B. Eyring once suggested that "You may have had the experience I have had of noticing that not very many people during a conversation listen carefully to the other person. Generally they are focusing on what they said last or what they will say next."[2]

Listening intently is one of the highest compliments that an individual can pay another person, but sadly, we often assume that we know what the other person is going to say before they say it. We cut each other off without letting the other person finish their thought. If we do allow them to finish their thought, we have usually already framed a response without fully understanding what they are actually saying. Most people, according to Steven R. Covey, "do not listen with the intent to understand; they listen with the intent to reply."[3]

If you listen to the other person without trying to frame your next sentence, you'll pick up on things that may help you resolve concerns that are underneath the surface. It tells them that you really care about what they're saying. When you look at them and give them your exclusive attention, your body language will show them that you're engaged. Nothing is more irritating than when you have something important to say and no one is listening.

People just want to feel important, and listening is the best way to make someone feel that way. A good listener is hard to come by. People love, respect, and trust a great listener.

Our kids ask lots of questions. Sometimes they ask so many questions that it can get annoying. But don't ever let that be the case. They won't ask you questions forever, and one day when they're all grown up, you'll wish they would ask you a few more of those innocent little questions.

Listening is the single most powerful way to get to know someone, especially your kids. BYU basketball star Marty Haws used basketball as an opportunity to teach his son about life. Morning after morning, Marty would get up with his son Tyler, who wanted to go down to the gym at six a.m. and practice shooting the basketball.[4] Marty gave this simple but powerful piece of advice to every dad that would like to get closer to his kids. He said, "If we can learn to rebound a little more and talk a little less, I think our kids would be a little better off."[5] This timeless advice extends much further than just to basketball. It is the foundation upon which a dad can create an atmosphere where his child is most comfortable opening up and talking to their dad. For Marty, it was rebounding for his son at six a.m. every morning. That was his special place. It was sacred ground for a father and son to communicate and bond. Tyler shot. Marty rebounded. For you and your son or daughter, it might be on the golf course, on a surfboard, or on a ski slope. But whatever that safe and comfortable atmosphere is for your kids, make sure that you are mentally there with them and ready to listen.

Elder M. Russell Ballard tells a story of days past when he was a young father. He reminds us that we need to be attentive and ready to listen to our kids at all ages—not just when they are older. "Our first little girl, when she was five, climbed up on my lap while I was reading the newspaper. She was telling me something important to her, and I was not paying attention. So she reached up her little hands, pulled down the newspaper, clasped my face in her little hands, looked me squarely in the eyes, and said, 'Daddy, you are not listening to me!' She was right—and I was wrong in not listening to her."[6]

Most of us have found ourselves in the same situation as Elder Ballard. For him, it was a newspaper. For us, it might be our phones or devices. But we can't allow distractions to affect our ability to truly listen to and give our full attention to our children. Become too distracted, and, soon enough, those children will go and find someone else that will listen to them, and you will have lost your opportunity to become their mentor and confidant as they grow up during their childhood years and into adulthood.

NOTES

1. Russell M. Nelson, "Listen to Learn," *Ensign*, May 1991.
2. Henry B. Eyring, "Child of Promise," *BYU Speeches*, May 4, 1986.
3. Stephen R. Covey, *The 7 Habits of Highly Effective People* (New York: Free Press, 2004), 239.
4. Greg Bennett, "The Haws basketball legacy: A dad, two boys and a ball," *Utah Valley Magazine*, November 12, 2012.
5. Marty Haws in "HomeSports: Leave a Legacy," YouTube video, 4:14, posted by "HomeSports," December 20, 2013, www.youtube.com/watch?v=caYjt7OsjPs.
6. M. Russell Ballard, "The Opportunities and Responsibilities of CES Teachers in the 21st Century" (Address to CES Religious Educators, Salt Lake Tabernacle, February 26, 2016); www.lds.org/broadcasts/article/evening-with-a-general-authority/2016/02/the-opportunities-and-responsibilities-of-ces-teachers-in-the-21st-century.

DADS WHO ARE EMOTIONALLY INTELLIGENT

Every man I meet is my master in some point, and in that I learn of him.

Emerson[1]

SOME DADS DEAL with a lot of opposition in their lives. But it's how they respond to that opposition that will dictate how they go down in their family's history books. Our ability to learn, to grow, and to adapt is what separates our success from our failure in our pursuit to become great dads.

We are surrounded by people that we can learn from. I've made it my life's ambition to become a "greatest hits" of all the good I see in others. I've learned that the key to self-mastery in this life is to observe others closely and to learn from them. Take the bad that you observe in them and discard it. Take the good that you observe in them and apply it. Over time, having applied all the good that you've observed in great people, you'll become a walking "greatest hits" of good principles and behaviors. This concept of adapting, learning, and growing is what enables a dad to help his own children become the best that they can be.

Displayed on our living room wall is a quote from President Gordon B. Hinckley that simply reads, "Try a little harder to be a little better."[2] If we do that and block out worldly influences, we will indeed become better. Around AD 321, a man named

Ammaron made an observation about the young boy, Mormon, who eventually ended up compiling and abridging the various sets of scriptures that had been passed down from dad to son throughout the years on the American continent. Ammaron told Mormon that he believed him to be a "sober child" and that he was "quick to observe" (Mormon 1:2).

I believe there is one attribute above all others that will help dads effectively reach the hearts of the children they have stewardship over. That attribute is emotional intelligence. When someone is emotionally intelligent, it means that they are quick to observe. The great Hall of Fame baseball player Yogi Berra said, "You can observe a lot by just watching."[3] Great dads pay attention and watch closely. They don't allow themselves to be oblivious. Instead, they can read a room and know exactly what to bring to the table and how to bring it. They are simultaneously empathetic and sympathetic. They are strong and stalwart in keeping to their standards, yet are able to adapt to situations, providing an atmosphere in which the best possible outcome can be reached. You will need this attribute as your kids grow and get older, and as you are required to understand their various personalities. Just being the "stubborn old you" will not enable you to get inside their heads and help them make crucial life-changing decisions.

When someone is emotionally intelligent, they are truly able to "mourn with those that mourn; yea, and comfort those that stand in need of comfort" (Mosiah 18:8–10). Christ, in my mind, was the most emotionally intelligent being to walk the earth. He was able to "succor his people" according to their needs because He was so quick to observe (Alma 7:12). He placed himself in the positions of others and truly walked in their shoes. I believe that this attribute, coupled with the principle of love, was what enabled Him to carry on for us in that lonely garden those many years ago.

We can seek to acquire the gift of emotional intelligence. We can learn to be quick to observe, and it will benefit every aspect of our lives in every situation. Being quick to observe will enable us to more effectively teach our family throughout the years.

NOTES

1. Ralph Waldo Emerson, "Greatness," in *The Complete Works of Ralph Waldo Emerson*, vol. 8 (New York and Boston: Houghton, Mifflin, 1904); www.bartleby.com/90/0810.html.
2. Gordon B. Hinckley, "We Have a Work to Do," *Ensign*, May 1995.
3. Nate Scott, "The 50 greatest Yogi Berra quotes," *USA Today: For the Win*, September 23, 2015.

DADS WHO STAND BY OUR SIDE

You may have to fight a battle
more than once to win it.
Margaret Thatcher[1]

WE'VE ALL HEARD of troubled teens that sometimes run away from home for all the wrong reasons. Jesus referred to these sons and daughters as "prodigal." (See Luke 15:11–32.) When they realize what they've done, the only thing that prohibits them from going back home is pride, or the fear of facing their parents (usually their dad). All of us have been "prodigal" in some way. We've all made mistakes and have had to make a conscious decision to come back to open arms. Sometimes that choice is not an easy one to make. Sometimes quitting seems like the only option. It's important that dads stay humble and keep their arms wide open and ready for a wayward child to return home. The humble, forgiving fatherly love is at the core of the gospel of Jesus Christ.

While Jesus was on the earth, He set out to teach us what it means to be a father, and the importance of "seek[ing] that which was lost" (Ezekiel 34:16). He descended into a relentless storm of persecution and pain in order to find and rescue each and every one of us as we lay spiritually lifeless on life's toughest of battlefields. As fathers, we have been given the perfect example on how to handle

DADS WHO STAY AND FIGHT

children who have strayed. Who among us would not want to do the same for our children?

Christ finds us on our darkest nights; when we've hit rock bottom and have nowhere to turn. Sometimes we lay there on the ground with only enough strength to whisper, "Help me." When He hears our plea for help, He finds us, sets us on His shoulders, and carries us to safety. He subsequently nourishes us back to spiritual consciousness. Once we've awoken from our slumber, He reminds us about our heavenly home and tells us how much we've been missed. He grips our shoulders with tears in His eyes and says, "Look! I've come a long way to get you. I love you and I'll always be here for you. Will you walk home with me? It's not too late." If we allow Him, He'll then walk with us so we don't get lost on the way back.

Sister Elaine S. Dalton told a story about a woman by the name of Florence Chadwick who was known for long-distance, open-water swimming.

> Florence loved a challenge, and she later attempted to swim between the coastline of California and Catalina Island—some 21 miles (34 km). On this swim she grew weary after swimming 15 hours. A thick fog set in that obscured the view of the coastline. Her mother was riding alongside her in a boat, and Florence told her mother that she didn't think she could finish. Her mother and her trainer encouraged her to continue, but all she could see was the fog. She abandoned her swim, but once inside the boat, she discovered she had quit within one mile (1.6 km) of the coastline. Later, when she was interviewed and asked why she had abandoned her swim, she confessed that it wasn't

the cold water and it wasn't the distance. She said, "I was licked by the fog.[2]

Sister Dalton then described Florence Chadwick's next attempt to swim between California and Catalina Island: "Once more, a thick fog set in. But this time, [Florence] kept going until she successfully reached the coastline. This time when she was asked what made the difference, she said that she kept a mental image of the coastline in her mind through the thick fog and throughout the duration of her swim."[3]

Christ helps us to remember who we are and what our destination is. He doesn't hold a grudge against us. To Him, the past is in the past and He wants to move forward. He stands by our side yoked as one. He helps us finish our race, endure to the end, weather our storms, and cut through the fog to accomplish our goals. In doing this, Christ gives us the perfect example of what a dad should do for his children. Sometimes it's standing there with open arms to console and receive them, and other times it's being in their boat to point out the way, to lift their heads, and to strengthen their hearts. It's *always* about standing by their side and never giving up on them.

NOTES

1. Margaret Thatcher quoted in David K. Hatch, comp., *Everyday Greatness* (Nashville, TN: Routledge Hill Press, 2006), 367.
2. Elaine S. Dalton, "Now Is the Time to Arise and Shine!," *Ensign*, May 2012.
3. Ibid.

DADS' ROLES

DADS WHO TAKE MARRIAGE ADVICE

You don't get harmony when
everybody sings the same note.
Doug Floyd[1]

I MET THE woman of my dreams fourteen years ago. I saw her for the first time at church and told myself I was going to marry her. That's pretty shallow of me, I know—but that's the truth. Hey, I was twenty-one! What can I say?

As we hung out, I wanted to marry her even more. She was smart, funny, and spiritual, and she had a great family. One day, we sat down with an older gentleman unrelated to us in any way who wanted to give us some marriage advice. My soon-to-be wife—being infinitely more humble than I was—listened eagerly to this old codger as he gave us what he considered "the best marriage advice" he could ever give. I sat there like the know-it-all twenty-one-year-old guy that I was and just "endured it" without giving it much thought. How could I have imagined how true his words would be? Yet here I am, these fourteen years later, calling it "the best piece of marriage advice I ever received."

"When you get married," said the man, "don't try to turn the other person into you." Simple enough, right?

But people have a natural tendency to think that everyone should see things the way they do. We're amazed and bewildered when someone disagrees with us. We think the person who disagrees with us must be crazy. We do this the most with the person that we marry. Many times we can't understand why the other person doesn't like the same things we do or why they don't understand our point of view on certain matters.

One day, not too long ago, I asked my wife if she'd like to go on a walk. It was cold and rainy outside. I personally love the rain, so I figured that she'd like walking in the rain as well. Nope. Not at all. When it's rainy, she likes to stay inside and get bundled up. But to me, wind, rain, and cold are fun. I gave her a hard time for it because I couldn't understand why she wouldn't want to go. I figured that if I liked it, why wouldn't she?

The answer? Because she's not me!

It's okay to not like the same things all of the time. It's okay that your wife doesn't enjoy that notoriously boring game of golf. It's okay if she doesn't want to watch the football game. Just let her be her. Unfortunately, we tend to have a hard time with this. We say things like, "Why don't you want to play golf with me?" or "How is it that you don't find football interesting?"

Regardless of how perfectly matched you think you are with your wife, there will always be disagreement. People are different. Men and women are especially different. Accept that and embrace it. Turn it into a positive.

A wise man by the name of Spencer W. Kimball gave the same advice when describing his own marriage to his wife Camilla. He used an oblong Venn diagram to describe his prescription for marital happiness. In the Venn diagram, he showed how there was plenty of overlap. These were things that Spencer and Camilla agreed about and enjoyed together. This overlapping section was the source of their greatest happiness. However, there were spaces

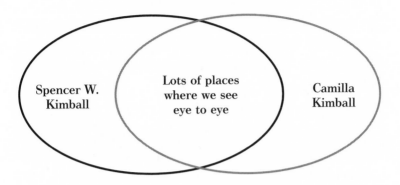

on the diagram where Spencer and Camilla didn't try to overlap. They learned not to even try to go there.[2] There are inevitably going to be places in a marriage where the two of you just won't overlap. That's okay! It's even healthy. You're different people, with different upbringings, from different cultures, with unique personalities. You'd probably hate life if you married someone identical to yourself because most of the time, the things that irritate you most about other people are things that you would inwardly recognize as your own flaws and weaknesses.

Here's the key: support each other in whatever endeavors the other person enjoys. Don't try to force the other person to enjoy what you enjoy. If you do that, neither of you will enjoy anything. You'll spend your time trying to change the other person and end up hitting your head against a block wall. It's painful. People never change because someone else wants them to. In fact, coercive change often causes revolt. People only change because of an inward desire to change.

President Gordon B. Hinckley once noted, "If there's anything that irritates me it's these men who try to run their wives' lives and tell them everything they ought to do and so on and so on."[3] At a conference, Marjorie Pay Hinckley confirmed that President Hinckley practiced what he preached, then told the congregation,

"I am very grateful for a husband who always lets me do my own thing. . . . He never insists that I do anything his way, or any way for that matter. From the very beginning he gave me space and let me fly. What a man!"[4]

That wise old dad was right those many years ago as he sat us down to give us advice before we became parents. "Don't try to turn the other person into you." Let them be them, and you be you, and then revel in the time you spend in the middle. Because when it's all said and done, the strength of your marriage will in large measure impact the efficacy of your fatherhood.

NOTES

1. Doug Floyd quoted in David K. Hatch, comp., *Everyday Greatness* (Nashville, TN: Routledge Hill Press, 2006), 301.
2. Truman G. Madsen, *Audio Talk Series: The Awesome Power of Married Love*, performed by Truman G. Madsen, Deseret Book, 2006, audio CD.
3. Doug Robinson, "Margorie Hinckley—'Every bit his equal'," *Deseret News*, April 5, 2003.
4. Ibid.

MAKE MOM

HAPPY

DADS WHO SERVE MOM

If you want something to last
forever, you treat it differently.
F. Burton Howard[1]

WHEN I LOOK back I can't believe it took me ten years to actually learn the great secret behind making my wife truly happy. That's like . . . longer than it takes to become a doctor. I'm probably exaggerating. I know I've made my wife happy over the years, but over time, I've noticed that our marriage doesn't always look like our dating years. I've had to relearn how to make her happy. To know the secret of unlocking your wife's happiness, you first need to know a few things about her. Provided that she's a good woman, she probably doesn't care about the things you think she cares about. You go into the business world every day thinking that if you can make tons of money she'll respect you more. You think that if you hit the gym every day and get six-pack abs that she'll somehow not be able to take her hands off of you. You think that if you hold "powerful" titles in the various organizations you're associated with that she'll brag about you to her friends and family.

To a good woman, all of these things mean nothing. She doesn't want your money, your muscles, or your titles. When you first met her, you probably had none of that (except maybe a few more muscles), and those were probably some of your happiest times. So what did you have going for you during those early dating years?

It's simple—you served her. You genuinely served her. You went out of your way to show her that you cared. You were constantly trying to win her heart. You made her feel special, and deep down, there's a good chance that your wife wants that more than anything else in this world. She wants to feel special to the person on this earth she cares most about. Mary Stewart Cutting said, "A woman can stand anything but being forgotten, not being needed."[2] Aren't we all that way? Don't we all have that innate desire to be important to someone?

I was talking to my wife recently, and I was telling her that I didn't think I correctly understood what serving her really meant. I've always felt like I've served her during our marriage. I help her when she asks me to fix the computer or printer. I work hard during the day for her and the kids. I take her out to dinner (normally with the kids). I say nice things to her on a regular basis. I take out the trash or help with things around the house. But as I thought about all of the things I do for her, I realized that most of the things I feel like I'm doing to serve her are actually just serving the family. Most of the things I do are no more than the necessary routines of life. I'd do them regardless of whether she's around or not. Most functions are just basic hygiene and maintenance factors for living.

When I go above and beyond my routine, without being prompted, to dip into the things that might be troubling her—that's when she really lights up. When I do the things she knows I really don't want to do at the times I don't want to do them—that is when she becomes a raving fan. At that point, sparks fly and other troubles seem to fade into the background.

There's so much untapped potential within every marriage. Many marriages fall apart because of a single principle: two people who were once madly in love forget what it means to truly serve one another. Unsolicited service at inconvenient times is the glue that holds relationships together. This type of service causes and enables a relationship to excel far beyond what it was even in those dating years. The more you serve someone, the more you love them.

For some reason, as my wife has explained to me, there is nothing that turns her on to me more than when I start cleaning the kitchen and dishes all by myself without being asked or prompted. It's just a little thing—and yet it remains among one of the most effective things I could have done during the day to make her crazy about me. Again, these are the types of things a person thinks of doing when they're dating, but once married life sets in and you succumb to the routines of life, you lose that unique sense of service. You fall into these mental ruts:

"I already do so much for everyone."

"I normally do this for the family, and you normally do that for the family."

"I do my job, and you do your job."

This mind-set has got to be one of the most unrecognized—and yet all too common follies of post-honeymoon married life. I've learned that I must transcend my comfortable routine and cease doing the bare minimum required to classify me as a "good husband." I don't want her to remember me as "good." I want to be remembered as "great" in her eyes and in the eyes of my children. Performing unexpected acts of service for my wife is like pouring gasoline on hot coals in a Southern California beach pit. These simple acts take me into another realm of happiness at home.

I can't believe it took me ten years to figure out this secret. Better late than never, I guess. It's a secret that is staring so many love-starved couples in the face, and it's really easy to implement once you witness the benefits of practicing it.

NOTES

1. F. Burton Howard, "Eternal Marriage," *Ensign*, May 2003.
2. Mary Stewart Cutting quoted in Stan Cronin, *How to Date Your Wife* (Springville, Utah: Horizon Publishers, 2004), 119.

DADS WHO HELP MOM FEEL BEAUTIFUL

The most important thing a father can do
for his children is to love their mother.
Theodore M. Hesburgh[1]

LIKE MOST LITTLE boys, I hung out with my mom a lot while I was growing up. She was full of these little one-liners that sounded like she'd just pulled them from a fortune cookie.

"Blossom where you're planted."

"Actions speak louder than words."

"You can judge a man's character by how he treats animals."

She had many others, but the one that always stuck out to me was, "Beauty is in the eye of the beholder."

Today's TV shows and movies depict women that have successful careers, workout regimens, and perfect bodies; women who have kids, raise kids, take care of kids, stay looking young, cook, clean, take care of the house, and much more. Unfortunately, these fictional depictions translate into real-life expectations. Conversely, there are very few expectations placed upon men in these shows, as they consistently break the heart of the woman who works so hard to be perfect for her man.

From an early age, many women have been set up to fail. Expectations have been stacked so high upon their shoulders that when they inevitably cannot live up to those expectations, they begin to doubt their self-worth. No woman can feel beautiful when she feels worthless.

We listen to these TV shows, sitcoms, and movies where various women are degraded and disrespected. While millions laugh and chuckle and cheer, a little girl somewhere is taking it all in, and a little boy is shaping his worldview of women. What we don't realize as a society is that it is our youth that are consuming this stuff more than anyone else. They see it on TV, they see it in the world, and sometimes they even see it in their own homes. It seems as if there cannot be a movie made without some sort of scandalous act of disloyalty and betrayal. It has become a staple in our society. We've come to expect it. No one feels safe in their relationships, and insecurity abounds.

I believe there is one thing above all else that a man can do for his kids that will impact their life more than anything else.

A man should make his wife (their mom) feel like the most beautiful woman in the world—and make sure his kids see it. He should go out of his way to make her feel appreciated. Make her feel like she is enough, and more than enough. Make his voice of positivity and encouragement in her ear become louder and more persistent than the world's voice. She will know that regardless of what the world says to her and regardless of how she feels about herself, she can always go to this man when she wants to feel beautiful. As the kids witness this, it will be the number one subconscious determinant for them as they then choose who to marry and how to act in that marriage.

A daughter will observe the way her dad treats her mom and will most likely select a man that has a similar temperament and disposition. Her decision will bless or curse her life. A son will also watch his dad and look up to him. What that son observes in his dad will most likely translate into how he treats his future wife. His actions in that marriage will bless or curse his life as well. So much happiness is found in the Doctrine and Covenants command to "cleave unto [your wife] and none else" To "cleave" means to "adhere firmly and closely or loyally and unwaveringly."[2] To the world, to "cleave" seems too old-fashioned, but it is the attribute of a man who knows how to make his wife feel beautiful.

There is no limit to the amount of love that can flow from a woman who feels confident and beautiful. So, not only will a man be doing himself a huge favor by making his wife feel beautiful, but he will be teaching his kids one of the most important lessons they can learn in this life—how to treat your wife (for sons), and how to pick a husband (for daughters). Truly, some of the best love stories ever told were the ones that persisted decades beyond what the world deems as beautiful: wrinkles and spots, shrinking and slumping, balding and bad eyesight. Yet, a real man, being the "beholder" of his wife, is still able to make her feel like the most beautiful woman in the world.

NOTES

1. "The most important thing a father can do for his children is to love their mother," *Somebody's Mother's*, January 19, 2017, www.somebodysmothers.com/lidlits/#/theodore-hesburgh.
2. *Merriam-Webster*, s.v., "cleave," January 31, 2017, www .merriam-webster.com/dictionary/cleave.

DADS AND DAUGHTERS

When my father didn't have my
hand . . . he had my back.
Linda Poindexter[1]

IF I WERE to ask a thousand dads to articulate in words the
love they have for their daughter, I bet each one of the them would
stumble and fumble at the very thought. The great British essayist
and playwright Joseph Addison said, "Certain is it that there is no
kind of affection so purely angelic as of a father to a daughter. In
love to our wives there is desire; to our sons, ambition, but to our
daughters there is something which there are no words to express."[2]

We often hear about the relationship between a mom and her
daughter. There is no doubt that those relationships are sweet, everlasting, essential, and important to the growth and development
of a daughter, but we should never underestimate the monumental role a father can and should play in his daughter's life. Sister
Elaine S. Dalton, in speaking to dads, said simply, "You are your
daughter's hero."[3]

A daughter will look to her mother on what to do, how to act,
how to look, and how to live. But a daughter will look to her dad
for core validation on everything that she is. Her person, her character, her accomplishments, and her direction in life will be largely
influenced by what her perceived value is to her dad. In my experience, a dad plays a critical role in the development of his daughter's

self-esteem or lack thereof. She is as she views herself through her father's eyes. Elder Jeffrey R. Holland once met a young Laurel at a conference assignment who subsequently wrote him a letter about her dad:

> I wish my dad knew how much I need him spiritually and emotionally. I crave any kind comment, any warm personal gesture. I don't think he knows how much it would mean to me to have him take an active interest in what is going on in my life, to offer to give me a blessing, or just spend some time together. I know he worries that he won't do the right thing or won't say the words well. But just to have him *try* would mean more than he could ever know. I don't want to sound ungrateful because I know he loves me. He sent me a note once and signed it 'Love, Dad.' I treasure that note. I hold it among my dearest possessions.[4]

It's been said that most women marry the spitting image of their dad. Your daughter is internalizing everything you do and everything you say over time. The crucial decision of who she eventually marries is based on a subconscious accumulation of a lifetime of observing the only man in her life: her dad. We'd better set the bar high so that she'll marry a man who feels the same way we do about her!

Dr. Meg Meeker, a well-known practicing pediatric and adolescent medical physician, has spent the last thirty years listening to the struggles, worries, and fears of young women and girls. Her experience and research suggests that the role a father plays in his daughter's life is the most influential factor in determining the lifelong happiness of a woman.

In the very beginning of her book *Strong Fathers, Strong Daughters*, Dr. Meeker pleads with men everywhere to step up to the plate for their daughters:

> Men, good men: We need you. We—mothers, daughters, and sisters—need your help to raise young women. We need every ounce of masculine courage and wit you own, because fathers, more than anyone else, set the course for a daughter's life.
>
> Your daughter needs the best of who you are: your strength, your courage, your intelligence, and your fearlessness. She needs your empathy, assertiveness, and self-confidence. She needs *you*.[5]

Much of the rest of Dr. Meeker's book goes on to substantiate her claim on the importance of fathers to their daughters with hard undeniable evidence. Before she gets into the data, she speaks to dads directly and makes an assertion that no father can ignore:

> When you come in the room, they change. Everything about them changes: their eyes, their mouths, their gestures, their body language. Daughters are never lukewarm in the presence of their fathers. They might take their mothers for granted, but not you. They light up—or they cry. They watch you intensely. They hang on your words. They hope for your attention, and they wait for it in frustration—or in despair. They need a gesture of approval, a nod of encouragement, or even simple eye contact to let them know you care and are willing to help.
>
> When she's in your company, your daughter tries harder to excel. When you teach her, she learns more rapidly. When you guide her, she gains confidence. If you fully understood just how profoundly you can influence

your daughter's life, you would be terrified, overwhelmed, or both. Boyfriends, brothers, even husbands can't shape her character the way you do. You will influence her entire life because she gives you an authority she gives no other man.[6]

If you don't have anything in common with your daughter, then get interested in what she likes. Take her on dates. Talk to her. Ask her questions. Build trust. Invest the time. Become her greatest fan, her biggest advocate. Show her exactly what it means to be a real man in a world where real men are few and far between. Show her the standard of excellence in men and she will blossom into a self-confident cornucopia of skills and goodness that lives up to the potential that is inside of her. Become a master of seeing, recognizing, and drawing out the best of her and she will honor you in everything that she does for the rest of her life.

NOTES

1. Linda Poindexter quoted in "When my father didn't have my hand . . . he had my back," Katie Mather, *Quote Catalog*, January 20, 2017, https://quotecatalog.com/quote/linda-poindexter-when-my-father-LaDE4k1.
2. Attributed to Joseph Addison.
3. Elaine S. Dalton, "Love Her Mother," *Ensign*, November 2011.
4. Jeffrey R. Holland, "The Hands of the Fathers," *Ensign*, May 1999; italics in original.
5. Meg Meeker, *Strong Fathers, Strong Daughters* (New York: Ballantine, 2007), 7; italics in original.
6. Ibid., 8.

COURAGEOUS
LOYAL
FAITHFUL
TRUE

DADS AND SONS

When I was little, I thought [my dad] was Superman. Now I know he's Superman.
Chad Lewis[1]

AS MUCH AS our daughters are influenced by what we think, our sons' entire lives will be impacted by what we do. Our sons watch every move we make, just as the Savior watched our Heavenly Father's every move. "The Son can do nothing of himself," the Savior said during His earthly ministry, "but what he seeth the Father do: for what things soever he doeth, these also doeth the Son likewise" (John 5:19).

Dads have many responsibilities, but none more important than the molding and shaping of their sons into true men: men of God, not men of the world—courageous, loyal, faithful, true, hardworking men!

It was Grit Young, father of Steve Young, who encouraged his downtrodden and defeated son to stick it out and not be a quitter.[2] Without Grit, Steve Young might not be the NFL legend and household name that he is today.

It was Bryant S. Hinckley who lovingly rebuked Gordon B. Hinckley for thinking too much of himself as a newly called missionary in a foreign land.[3] Without Hinckley, the father, we probably wouldn't have ever known Hinckley, the son, as the prophet and president of The Church of Jesus Christ of Latter-day Saints.

It was Lehi, who was willing to leave all that he had worked for behind in order to follow the Lord's command and "[dwell] in a tent" (1 Nephi 2:15), that led Nephi to be the kind of son that "will go and do" (1 Nephi 3:7) instead of "sit and stew."[4]

It was Alma who taught Helaman to have "an everlasting hatred against sin" (Alma 37:32) and to "never be weary of good works" (Alma 37:34). It was Alma who taught his son Shiblon to "not [be] lifted up unto pride" (Alma 38:11) and to "bridle his passions" (Alma 38:12). And it was Alma who said to his son Corianton that he should "have tended to the ministry wherewith [he] wast entrusted" (Alma 39:4).

As Alma was recounting his own repentance and conversion to his son Helaman, Alma gave credit to his own dad, saying, "I remembered also to have heard my father prophesy unto the people concerning the coming of one Jesus Christ, a Son of God, to atone for the sins of the world" (Alma 36:17). Alma went on to explain that it was the memory of his father teaching about the Atonement of Christ that caused him to cry out to God for repentance and forgiveness. That moment changed Alma's life forever (Alma 18–24).

It's a father's job to set the example for his son in all that he does. His work ethic, his worship, and his willingness to serve others will do more for his son than anything else. It's hard to describe the look I see in my son's eyes as he looks at me. It's as if he is continually asking me to lead him, love him, and endorse him. He wants me as a friend, an advocate, a leader, and a teacher. Elder M. Russell Ballard might have said it best when he said, "There is no other relationship quite like that which can and should exist between a boy and his dad."[5]

This relationship, if nurtured, can become an unspoken brotherhood, a vow, and an understanding that father and son must stick together in order to become protectors of all that is good in the world: we must respect and defend women and children; we must step up to help the hungry and the homeless; and we should, above all, love God and keep His commandments in a world that is discarding God as a relic of the past.

The son I raise should be the kind of son you hope your daughter will find, and that is not an easy task. At the end of the day, we raise our sons to protect and defend someone else's daughters in a way that we wish for our own daughters to be protected. We want our sons to preside, provide, and protect their own little families so that, one day, they will be esteemed, held up, revered, and remembered by those that call them "Dad."

NOTES

1. Chad Lewis in "HomeSports: Leave a Legacy," YouTube video, 4:14, posted by "HomeSports," December 20, 2013, www.youtube.com/watch?v=caYjt7OsjPs.
2. LeGrande Young in "HomeSports: Leave a Legacy," YouTube video, 4:14, posted by "HomeSports," December 20, 2013, www.youtube.com/watch?v=caYjt7OsjPs.
3. "Sweet Is the Work: Gordon B. Hinckley, 15th President of the Church," *New Era*, May 1995.
4. John Bytheway, *5 Scriptures that will Motivate You to Action*, performed by John Bytheway, Deseret Book, 2012, audio CD.
5. M. Russell Ballard, "Fathers and Sons: A Remarkable Relationship," *Ensign*, November 2009.

JOSEPH

ADOPTED
FATHER
OF THE
SAVIOR

DADS WHO ADOPT

For as I had ever called them my sons (for they were all of them very young) even so they said unto me: Father, behold our God is with us, and he will not suffer that we should fall.

Helaman, to his adopted sons[1]

OVER THE PAST few years, I have become fascinated by the concept of adoption. After my wife and I were married, we were blessed with two children very quickly. Taylor came first, just over ten months from the day we were married, and Trenton followed just fifteen months after Taylor was born. All of a sudden, four years had gone by and we were unable to get pregnant with a third child—until one day, my wife, Kristyn, was finally pregnant. Almost immediately after we found out that she was pregnant, she got sick with a fever, higher than anything she had previously experienced in her life. The fever was so high that she lost the child in a miscarriage. Kristyn was devastated. After multiple doctors' opinions, we concluded that she was indeed done having biological children of her own.

I couldn't help but wonder why God would allow this to happen to such a good mother while there are so many other women out there that can have babies at the drop of a hat, and some of these mothers don't even want children. So many babies are born out of wedlock, or are aborted, discarded, or given away, and here was a loving mother just waiting for Heavenly Father to send His precious spirits to her. I couldn't understand it.

We were lucky. We were given two beautiful kids before Kristyn's reproductive abilities were gone, so we have nothing to complain about. But what about all of the great moms and dads out there who have waited their entire lives to become parents, but have been denied the ability to bring a child into this world with no hope in sight? The burden of that reality has been more than some could bear. I can't know what it's like for a woman to desire a child, but I do know what it's like to be a man with the desire to be called "Dad." When you're being denied that opportunity, what are the options?

This is where my fascination with adoption comes in. As I've studied the doctrine behind adoption, I've come to realize that God doesn't distinguish between biological and adopted children. In the light of the gospel, we're all brothers and sisters who have been given stewardship over our other brothers and sisters, in order to learn how to become heavenly parents ourselves.

I've come to realize that adoption is at the center of the entire gospel of Jesus Christ. It is woven into everything that we practice and believe. It is prevalent throughout both the Old and New Testaments and was utilized even by Heavenly Father Himself with His firstborn spirit child and Only Begotten Son in the flesh.

Because I've never experienced what it's like to adopt, I reached out to a good friend of mine who has embraced adoption and fully experienced the blessings that flow from it. Brandon Doman was a BYU star quarterback and a Heisman trophy candidate, was drafted into the NFL by the San Francisco 49ers, and was an offensive coordinator for BYU football.[2] Because of various business ventures I've had with him, I've been able to get to know him as a man and a dad, instead of as the "Domanator" who throws footballs.[3] He wouldn't tell you this, but in recent years, Brandon has received multiple collegiate head coaching offers, all of which he has turned down out of a desire to spend more time with his wife and six kids.

What most people don't realize is that all of Brandon's kids are adopted. To Brandon, he is their dad, just as much as if they were biologically his. He loves them and wants to be with them. He wants to have the time to be at their events, to support them, and to see them grow into successful adults. I'm not saying that anyone who coaches a team doesn't care about their kids, but what I am saying is that for Brandon and his wife, Alisha, they want to spend as much time as possible with their family. They didn't have to adopt. They could have chalked it up as bad luck and moved on to focus on their careers. Instead, they made the decision to apply the godly attribute of adoption to their lives and build a family that is no different than yours or mine. Brandon made the decision to bypass lucrative and promising offers and give up the game he loved so much to spend more time with the six kids he loved even more. The guy lives and breathes football. He's a winner and a competitor. The smell of the leather, the touch of the grass, the roar of the crowd, and the brotherhood that exists among players is something that he'll never forget. But these kids that he took under his wing became his team, and he became their coach. He said very humbly, "I feel as though my wife and I have been blessed beyond measure to have the six children that we do. We feel as though they have blessed our lives far more than we could ever bless theirs. Adoption is a miraculous selfless act that brings families together in a very direct and inspired way."[4]

I asked Brandon how he developed such a view on adoption when so many people struggle with the concept. He indicated that his faith and understanding of God's plan of salvation gave him and his wife the direction and strength needed to apply the scriptural concept of adoption to their family. As he made these life-changing decisions, he said, "We draw great strength from Joseph, the adopted father of the Savior. His love and devotion to Mary and willingness to commit his life to earthly fatherhood granted to him by Heavenly Father allowed him to be the earthly patriarch for the Savior."[5] It was the God of heaven, the most powerful being in this universe, who utilized the principle of adoption to bring forth and raise the Son of God.

Brandon summarized his thoughts on adoption by saying:

> Heavenly Father seals upon us the promised blessings of Abraham, Isaac, and Jacob, regardless of whether we are born in the covenant or adopted into the covenant. It doesn't matter how we find the promised blessings of the sealing covenant. What matters is that we find it. We believe that adoption has afforded those blessings to our children. We are confident that this was guided by a loving Heavenly Father who knows the design and outcome of our existence.[6]

This thought intrigued me because it is consistent with the doctrine of sealing families—a doctrine that ranks among the sweetest of doctrines to be restored in these latter days. But sometimes, we misunderstand that doctrine. We have this vision of our family sealed together, where young kids stay young and we continue being their parents throughout eternity. What we sometimes fail to see is that the most important sealing that takes place is between husband and wife. It will be the same for your children and their children. They will get married and be sealed to their spouse, whereupon they will have the opportunity to seal biological or adopted children back to God by sealing those children to them. The sealing of children to parents is really designed to seal those children back to their Heavenly Parents. The earthly parents, regardless of who they are, and as long as they are worthy, become the link or conduit through which children are bound, or grafted, back into the eternal family of our Heavenly Parents. This sealing to our Heavenly Parents enables us to dwell in the celestial kingdom with the rest of our family members who have been found worthy to abide in that glory. In the celestial kingdom, we are also promised that each of us will be able to utilize the creative powers we witness in our Heavenly Parents.

Jeremy Jergensen, a good friend of mine and a busy stake president, talked about his faith being a central part of his and his wife Liz's decision to adopt. Without his faith and understanding of families, they might have overlooked their miraculous opportunity to adopt and would be "missing the two sweet little spirits whom we love so much."[7] For Jeremy's wife, Liz, she said simply, "My faith has been everything throughout the adoption process."[8] Because of the Restoration of the gospel, adoption takes on a whole new meaning and significance. Before the sealing keys were restored, all of us were children without parents. But now, each of us has the opportunity to be brought together through the binding power of the Atonement. Jeremy told me, "The greatest blessing of the entire adoption process was to enter the House of the Lord [the temple] and have a child who was not born in the covenant be sealed to you."[9] That act on the part of two loving adoptive parents brought two adopted kids into the family of God with an eternal promise to never be fatherless again.

The Lord does all of His important work through proxies. Christ was a proxy for us. We are proxies for our deceased ancestors in the saving ordinances of the temple. Earthly parents are proxies for Heavenly Parents in our respective homes. Each proxy situation is designed to reconnect estranged children back to their original parents—their Heavenly Parents. All of us have been asked to be proxies in some way, shape, or form in the same way that Joseph (Christ's adopted father) was asked to "stand in" for our Heavenly Father here on earth. Can you believe the trust bestowed upon each of us by our Heavenly Father? The principle of adoption is woven into every facet of the gospel, and the dad that becomes a father to the fatherless should be classed among the noblest of men found upon the earth.

NOTES

1. Alma 56:46.
2. "Brandon Doman Staff Bio," *The Official Home of the BYU Cougars*, January 20, 2017, byucougars.com/staff/m-football /brandon-doman.
3. "Brandon Doman and the Dominator Basketball Hoop," *HomeSports*, January 20, 2017, www.homesports.com /basketball-news/brandon-doman-dominator-basketball-hoop.
4. Brandon Doman, personal correspondence with author.
5. Ibid.
6. Ibid.
7. Jeremy Jergensen, personal correspondence with author.
8. Liz Jergensen, personal correspondence with author.
9. Jeremy Jergensen, personal correspondence with author.

DAD'S GOLDEN YEARS

You have a lifetime to work,
but children are only young once.
Polish Proverb

A COUPLE OF years ago, I sat down to have lunch with a business acquaintance to talk about some specific items regarding this man's business. He was about my same age and had a few kids who were a couple years younger than mine. What started out as a business meeting turned into a discussion on fatherhood that left us both in a quandary. We simultaneously asked each other why it is that so many dads our age spend so much time obsessing about work during what we considered "the golden years"—we defined those golden years as the years in which our kids are young and excited to be around us. We wondered why it has become a societal norm for dads to be gone so much in order to "further their career" or "build a nest egg." Why they are virtually willing to sacrifice anything and everything to get ahead in this world during the years that their kids are growing up. We wondered why more dads don't wait until their kids are grown and independent before they go out and try to conquer the world.

Now I know the standard answers to those questions.

"We've got to earn money for retirement."

"We've got to save up for the kids' college funds."

"I've got to work hard now while my body can still handle it."

"I just don't have a choice. I've got to put food on the table and my employer demands a crazy workload!"

It's for these reasons, and many others, that we bust our tails during our twenties, thirties, and forties, and they are valid and noble reasons for being a distracted dad during those important years. No one will fault the dad who goes out and leaves it all on the field for his family. I've been there, and I'm there right now. During our lunch, my friend and I ended up pointing the finger back at ourselves.

As my friend and I continued to talk, we came to the conclusion that most of us are required to work hard for our families during these golden years, but maybe we're not working as smart as we could. Maybe we allow ourselves to unnecessarily and unproductively obsess over our work. I sat there at this lunch appointment thinking about how I have so consistently allowed myself to become distracted with all of the other things I've got to do in life, while the most important thing I should be doing is giving my whole soul, my entire being, and my undivided attention to my wife and kids. But I often end up saying something like,

"Hold on, guys. Let me answer this email. It's real important; I'll be right there."

I didn't *have* to answer that email. There are rarely work emergencies that are truly worthy of interrupting quality family time.

There are very few dads out there that could claim that they were busier than Mitt Romney. Mitt earned a BA from Brigham Young University, as well as a JD and an MBA from Harvard. He led Bain Capital, one of the most successful private equity investment firms in the nation. He served as a bishop, a stake president, the governor of Massachusetts, the CEO of the Salt Lake Organizing Committee for the 2002 Winter Olympics, and came within inches of becoming the president of the United States.[1] The guy was just flat-out busy. But look at how Mitt's wife, Ann, describes Mitt as a father during these golden years. Regardless of what was going on in Mitt's professional life, Ann said, "Mitt would walk in the door after work, leave the briefcase at the door, that was it. Never thought about work again until he left in the morning. And we would just play, and enjoy each other, and enjoy the children."[2]

We don't need to answer "one last" email, send "one last" text, or "take that important call," while our son or daughter is tugging on our shirt to come and shoot some hoops with them. Not too long ago, there was a day when there were no emails, texts, or cell phones ringing in our ears and vibrating in our pockets. John Dye, the principal social media and influencer marketing strategist at Bonneville Communications, gave me his thoughts on a dad's golden years. He said, "Enjoy each moment. Even the toughest ones. Moments are the stuff memories are made of. So, don't rush back to work after a mid-afternoon concert or game for a child. Take the family out for ice cream afterward. And don't stay later than necessary at work to do something that could be done later. You can never make a more indelible mark on the world than the mark you make on the lives of your family members. So enjoy each moment and create memories!"[3]

A good friend of mine, who was a very successful corporate executive, told me that he felt so strongly that he needed to dedicate more time to his wife and kids that it drove him to leave his corporate success behind. He said he needed to "make a shift in [his] career when [he] was forty because [he] felt strongly that [he] needed to be more hands on with respect to [his] family." He suggested to me that, "We need to pick careers that enable us to be engaged and involved with our kids, which is why I made this huge change in my career 16+ years ago. I needed to have more control over my time," he said, "and I needed to be local. It was a huge decision [and a risky one at that,] but in retrospect it was the best thing we ever did."[4]

Some of us spend the entire first twenty years of our children's lives with our heads down and our noses to the grindstone. We feel the window of productive working years closing quickly with every day that goes by. But do we pause and ask ourselves whether the evermore important productive parenting years are slipping through our very fingers? Do we really need the things we think we need? Will the extra hours, the extra cars, and the extra clothes be worth it in the end if we have to sacrifice the most important years of our kid's childhood to get them?

In my business career, I've had to take many risks. At various times, those risks have consumed me. I've thought to myself that I needed to work every waking minute in order to make things work. But what I didn't realize was that I was depriving myself of the balance I needed in order to operate at higher efficiency levels—both at work and at home. At times in the past, I've been almost paralyzed with the fear of not being able to provide for my family. I've lost sleep over the thought of being a failure and an embarrassment to my family. I've asked my wife on multiple occasions if she will still love me if I'm able to do nothing more than put food on the table. And do you know what she says? She tells me that all she really cares about is that we're together as a family: not the car, not the clothes, not the house. Just us, moving forward together.

I'm still required to take risks in business, but one risk I refuse to take is the risk of letting these golden years go by without being an active and integral part of my family's life. When the Book of Mormon prophet Jacob knew that his days were coming to an end, he said something that each of us can quickly identify with: "our lives passed away like as it were unto us a dream" (Jacob 7:26). Our time here is so short, and when we come to the end of our earthly road, we're going to wish above all else that we had been present and involved with our families during those golden years.

NOTES
1. "A Love Story," YouTube video, 3:43, posted by "mittromney's channel," March 3, 2012, www.youtube.com /watch?v=cRqW0VodVAU.
2. *Wikipedia*, s.v., "Mitt Romney," last modified January 23, 2017, en.wikipedia.org/wiki/Mitt_Romney.
3. John Dye, Facebook correspondence with author.
4. Mark McKell, email correspondence with author.

THE DAD RULES

DAD'S BIGGEST FEAR

Children are not things to be molded,
but are people to be unfolded.

Jess Lear[1]

IF YOU THOUGHT you worried a lot before you became a dad—just wait. I never knew what true worry was until I became a dad. Sure, I had various situations that made me fearful and apprehensive in my life, but from the minute I had those little souls placed under my stewardship, my worries compounded exponentially. But, so did my joy and sense of purpose.

People always fear the things they can't control. Every dad knows that they can never truly control their kids. Maybe they can rein them in when they are young, but once they mature and start claiming their God-given freedom, all you can do is hope that you've trained them in such a way that leads them to make good decisions with their life.

A dad's biggest fear consists of a desire for his kids to live up to—not fall short of—their divine potential. He doesn't want to see his kids suffer from making bad decisions, or see them leave an opportunity to attain happiness. But some dads think that they can micromanage their way into raising perfect kids. Sometimes a father loves his kids so much that he tries to force them into lifestyle choices that he believes will make his kids happy and successful. We've seen it all before; a dad gets it in his head that his son or daughter should go to such and such a school, play such and such a sport, or master such and such an instrument. He's determined that the best course of action for his child is for them to become a doctor or a lawyer, a dentist or an accountant. He goes to great lengths to set up a career path that will meet his expectations. He does all of this out of love, but also out of fear. He fears that his innocent, ignorant, and immature child will not make the sort of choices that will lead them to happiness, and therefore, this dad will step in and effectually pave the way to what he perceives as success. But what if the dad's perception of happiness is completely different from his child's perception of happiness? His assumptions and coercions could prove counterproductive, even disastrous, in the life of that child.

Similarly, we've all seen dads who try to live through their kids. They push them so hard that the kids forget to enjoy the activity that they once loved. All you need to do is head out to your local baseball fields to find a host of "little league dads" who are belligerently trying to make up for what they lacked in talent when they were young or relive their own glory days. I've watched good kids stand there and watch their dads get into fights with other dads and umpires over trivial things. This sort of behavior ends up making their kids' lives miserable and drives a wedge of resentment between the father and the child—resentment that doesn't manifest itself until the child has grown. At that point, the damage is done and the reversal of those feelings is difficult.

I grew up playing competitive baseball from ages four to twenty-two, until I served a mission—leaving behind a college scholarship and some interest from some major league scouts on the table. I always thought my son would also end up playing competitive baseball and be just like his old man (but better). I figured it would be "in his blood" to pick ground balls, steal bases, and hit gap shots. I would get so amped up when I'd see him get out there on that mound and strike people out. At age seven, he made his little league all-star team—and then innocently let me know that he didn't care whether he played ball or not. I never wanted to be one of those dads who drove his kids to do something that they didn't want to do. Now he plays the violin and the guitar; he swims, surfs, and performs with the world-class Millennial Choirs and Orchestras—and he's loving life. Do I still lose my mind at the smell of a baseball glove, the crack of a bat, or the feeling of freshly cut grass and neatly dragged dirt? Of course I do. But it doesn't come close to seeing his beaming face sing his heart out and bless others with music in the various concert halls across America.

The key is to create a happy medium, in which we're not forcing our kids into living the life that we think they should live. It's giving our kids the tools to help them gravitate toward the things that they are good at. The things they enjoy. The things that they want to excel at and share with the world. It does no good to force a mathematician to be an artist, an entrepreneur to be dentist, or a soccer player to be a golfer. Sometimes the fear we have over how our children will turn out can actually hurt them instead of help them to succeed. So, we should give them opportunities to find themselves, and then we stand by their side, ready to give counsel along the way. Whatever they choose to do, it does no good to criticize them for it. It will only cause them to want to do that thing more. So instead, we should make sure to support, enjoy, and encourage them in their endeavors for as long as they will allow us to stand by their side.

NOTES

1. Jess Lear quoted in Dr. Stephen Briers, *How Your Child Thinks* (Pearson, 2008), 3.

DADS AND FOUNTAINS

No misfortune is so bad that whining
about it won't make it worse.
Elder Jeffrey R. Holland[1]

YOUR KIDS ARE watching you and listening to every word you say—and they'll be all over you the minute you slip up. When your kids are young and impressionable, what you say is gospel to them. One of my personal mottoes is "While you're whining, I'm working." Sometimes we get so caught up in the inequality and unfairness of life that we spend more time complaining about our circumstances than actually working to change them. The most prevalent indication that you're hanging out with a loser is based on their propensity to complain. Complainers rarely make things better—and almost always make things worse.

Many of us have a hard time controlling what comes out of our mouths. The Savior on one occasion said, "Not that which goeth into the mouth defileth a man; but that which cometh out of the mouth, this defileth a man" (Matthew 15:11). Sometimes I don't think we understand the importance of what He's saying here. Your words are one of the most significant determinants of your character.

When I was playing baseball in college, I had a coach say something to me that I'll never forget. I think I'd been complaining about something in the dugout when this coach came up to me.

"Greg," he said, "there are two types of people in this life: there are fountains and there are drains. Which one are you?" He later told me that he took that saying from an old-time hustler of a ball player named Rex Hudler.[2] Rex Hudler is the epitome of optimism, and people love to be around him. Fountains are continually springing up, giving life and happiness to everyone who surrounds them. Drains, on the other hand, sit in the dark corners hiding from sight, always taking and never giving. They grow moldy, and people might trip over them, unnoticed and incognito. No one ever takes a picture of a drain to remember for later. But fountains . . . fountains are framed and remembered for years to come.

This one concept is probably the most valuable thing I ever got from the game of baseball. I've thought to myself on many occasions, "Am I a fountain or a drain?" Sometimes I catch myself being a drain. During those times, I've recognized that I'm unhappy. When I turn myself into a fountain, I recognize that I become happy. It's that simple.

Unfortunately, this world is full of drains. It takes less effort to be a drain and let the fountains do all of the giving. These drains spend every second of every day looking for an i to dot and a t to cross. They have no desire to dot their own i's or cross their own t's, but they won't fail to point out i's and t's of others. They can't help but find fault, criticize others, and bring people down to their level in life. With a fit of rage or a slip of the tongue, they destroy what takes years to build. It's almost as if they're just waiting for something to happen that they can "go off" on. They treat each bad situation in life as if it were a personal attack and think everyone involved is trying to injure them. It's an "I'll show them" attitude, constantly drawing that daily line in the sand, waiting, just waiting, for someone to cross over (or even come close to) that line so that they can lash out. As President Gordon B. Hinckley once said, "There is nothing that dulls a personality so much as a negative outlook."[3]

But it goes beyond just being someone that no one wants to be around. Our words can cause serious damage in the lives of the people we love the most. Wisdom from the Apocrypha states, "The stroke of the whip maketh marks in the flesh: but the stroke of the tongue breaketh the bones."[4] People will remember the things you say, and they may never be able to forget. Wounds to the body heal quickly, but wounds to the soul can linger forever. Our words are often the leading indicator on whether we'll be forever classified as a fountain or a drain.

We should work hard to be uplifting to our wife and kids. They will hang on to every word, and unfortunately, our human condition causes us to hang onto the negative words more than the positive ones. We can make-or-break a marriage or a childhood merely by the things that consistently come out of our mouth. We can't hang our hats on the excuse that we were angry or that we lost our minds. While those excuses may be valid, they won't change the fact that "I said what I said, and there is nothing I can do to take it back." World wars, bloody battles, and tragic family estrangements through the ages have many times been the result of a few untimely words. Paul told the Ephesians to "Let no corrupt communication proceed out of your mouth, but that which is good to the use of edifying" (Ephesians 4:29).

We should try to "speak with the tongues of . . . angels" (1 Corinthians 13:1), and always remember that "a soft answer turneth away wrath" (Proverbs 15:1). Dads who truly understand this truth aren't putting others down, gossiping, or murmuring every time they open their mouths. They are lifting, blessing, and encouraging.

James gives some of the best advice found in the Bible when he says:

> For in many things we offend all. If any man offend not in word, the same is a perfect man, and able to bridle the whole body.
>
> Behold, we put bits in the horses' mouths, that they may obey us; and we turn about their whole body.
>
> Behold also the ships, which though they be so great, and are driven of fierce winds, yet are they turned about with a very small helm, whithersoever the governor listeth.
>
> Even so the tongue is a little member, and boasteth great things. Behold, how great a matter a little fire kindleth!
>
> And the tongue is a fire, a world of iniquity: so is the tongue among our members, that it defileth the whole body, and setteth on fire the course of nature; and it is set on fire of hell.
>
> For every kind of beasts, and of birds, and of serpents, and of things in the sea, is tamed, and hath been tamed of mankind:
>
> But the tongue can no man tame; it is an unruly evil, full of deadly poison. (James 3:2–8)

This is something that will challenge even the best of us. But to become the perfect men, the perfect dads, or the flowing fountains we'd like to become, we've got to control our tongues. Dads who drink of the living water—meaning that they live and love the gospel—will find that they become what Christ called "a well of water springing up" (John 4:14) as they bless and uplift others by the words that come out of their mouths. Everyone wants to be around a fountain. Everyone loves a fountain. So become one, and be loved.

NOTES

1. Jeffrey R. Holland, "The Tongue of Angels," *Ensign*, May 2007.
2. "Splinters—A Memoir by Rex Hudler," *Rex Hudler*, January 20, 2017, rexhudler.com/index.php/splinters.
3. Gordon B. Hinckley, "Forget Yourself," *BYU Speeches*, March 6, 1977.
4. Ecclesiasticus 28:17

TREAT
OTHERS
THE WAY THAT
THEY
WOULD LIKE TO
BE TREATED

DADS WHO LIVE BY THE PLATINUM RULE

Respect is love in action.
Bangambiki Habyarimana[1]

MANY OF US go through life believing in the Golden Rule, which states that we should treat others the way that we would like to be treated. This rule is a good rule. It will help most of us to at least be mindful of how we're treating others and cause us to strive to be better. But one day, I came across a man who told me of another rule. He called it the Platinum Rule. This rule, he said, seems to work better than the Golden Rule when it comes to close familial relationships.

The Golden Rule operates successfully under the assumption that everyone else wants to be treated the same way that you would like to be treated. The Platinum Rule turns the Golden Rule on its head. The Platinum Rule suggests that you should treat others the way that *they* would like to be treated. This rule requires that I first try and understand how someone would like to be treated, instead of assuming that their needs are identical to mine.

Your wife, your son, your daughter—they are all very different from you. The household that my wife grew up in was very different than the household I grew up in. In my house growing up, the way we showed love was to make fun of and joke with each other. My dad and I would play games of bloody knuckles and dead arm. Weird, right? But that was the way it was and I loved it. So naturally, that's what I'm used to. But my wife's family had a completely different way of doing things; they were much more proper with each other.

You may be really vocal in praising your wife and think you're doing her a great service, but maybe that's not what satisfies her. You say all of those things to her because that is how you'd like to be treated and you assume that she'd liked to be treated that way as well. You want her to praise you and vocally reinforce her love for you. That is how *you* might want to be treated. But maybe fewer words and more actions make her happy.

Maybe you grew up playing sports, but you have a son or a daughter who prefers music. Maybe they don't want to go to baseball games and eat peanuts and hot dogs. Just because I grew up liking baseball, doesn't mean my kids are going to enjoy a night at the ballpark. The Platinum Rule helps us look beyond ourselves and into the hearts of those we love, so that we can treat them the way that they would like to be treated.

NOTES

1. Bangambiki Habyarimana, *Pearls of Eternity* (Smashwords Edition, 2016).

DADS AS
COACHES

At the end of the day, I'm very convinced that
you're going to be judged on how you are as
a husband and as a father, and not on
how many bowl games [you] won.
Urban Meyer, Ohio State head coach[1]

I HAVE BEEN on various teams for almost my entire life. Each of the teams that I played for had a coach. I don't ever remember being a part of a winning team that had a bad coach, and I don't ever remember being on a bad team with a good coach. Good coaches always seem to find a way to succeed at making their players better as individuals and better as a collective unit. These good coaches over the years have taught me some of the most important lessons I've learned in life. When you're on a team, your team often becomes like a family to you. Oftentimes the coach is looked up to as a father figure to their players. I've been able to observe my coaches very closely over the years, and I've noticed one key attribute above all else that defines a good coach from a bad coach.

Good coaches see what other people don't. They focus on aspects of the game that are not very exciting to watch from a fan's perspective. For the majority of my sporting career, I played baseball. A number of people, including my wife, can't stand to watch baseball being played, but I've always loved the symbolic imagery behind the game of baseball. In baseball, the whole purpose is to get your team home. You win together, as a team, when you help your teammates make it back home. It was the worst thing in the world for us to leave any of our teammates stranded on base. Our goal was to "bring 'em home," when players were on base. Anything short of that was devastating to us.

In order to get our teammates home, the great coaches I've had taught me about sacrifice. They didn't focus on the more glamorous aspects of the game, such as hitting a home run. In fact, the good coaches I had didn't care much about home runs at all. If they happened, great, but they didn't get too excited about them. But when one of us laid down a perfectly executed sacrifice bunt to move one of our players closer to home plate, that's when my good coaches got excited. When I'd crowd the plate and take a fastball to the ribs in order to get on base or move a player over, that's when my good coaches were impressed. When I took an inside pitch and drove the ball to the right side of the field to move our guy from second to third, or when I hit a sacrifice fly ball to deep right field to bring the winning run home, that's what brought pride to the heart of the good coach. None of those scenarios would help a hitter's stats. While everyone was giving high fives to the teammate who made it home because of my sacrifice, I was trotting slowly back to the dugout. But while everyone was slapping hands with the teammate who represented the winning run, the good coach was in my face, proud as could be, letting me know that he "saw me workin'" and appreciated the unselfish play.

Good coaches always seem to value the little things that cause the great things to happen. They value and teach consistency. Instead of cheering for the person carrying the football into the end zone, they're cheering for the person who sacrificed his body and laid down a key block forty yards back. Instead of running to hug the guy who just scored the three-point shot for the win, the good coach runs to the guy who set a timely pick that enabled the open shot to be taken in the first place. You see, these good coaches are suckers for the small things. They don't care if you're a superstar or the worst guy on the team. Good coaches always recognize and reward the things that are done under the radar for the greater good of the team.

So, what kind of coach do you want to be for your family?

NOTES

1. Urban Meyer in Tom Limbert, *Dad's Playbook: Wisdom for Fathers from the Greatest Coaches of All Time* (San Francisco: Chronicle Books, 2012), 114.

M▢DERATION

DADS AND TECHNOLOGY

Technology is a useful servant,
but a dangerous master.
Christian Lange[1]

A FEW YEARS ago, my family and I took a trip to Yosemite National Park. We allowed our kids to play games on their devices while we drove long distances because over nine hours of driving can get pretty boring. As parents, we get that. We were kids once, and we didn't have those same devices so we resorted to asking our parents over and over again, "Are we there yet?" As a young kid on the same road trip, I spent my time sleeping, finding a way to annoy my sister, or staring at the barren brown desert for hours on end. When we finally reached that majestic Yosemite Valley, I was in awe. I'm still in awe as I enter that valley these many years later.

So I figured that when I announced to my kids, "We're here! We've finally arrived in Yosemite!" they would burst at the seams with excitement like I did when I was young. It didn't happen. I was driving our truck, trying as hard as I could to concentrate on the road and simultaneously gape at the artfully constructed lakes, rivers, waterfalls, and, of course, the famed "Half Dome." Guess what my kids were doing? Heads down, busy playing on their iPads. I almost gagged at the thought.

But here's the scariest part of it all. It would have been one thing if they were just so enthralled in what they were doing that they didn't know it was time to pay attention to the scenery. But when I told them that we were in Yosemite, they picked their heads up, said a few descriptive adjectives such as "awesome" and "cool," and then before I knew it, their heads were buried back in the games they were playing on their devices. I couldn't believe it. I was bewildered. How could this be? The first time my kids see Yosemite, they only take a few glances, make minor observations, and go back to their devices. It was then that I knew that I had to make a change.

The thing we need to keep in mind is that none of this is their fault. It's my fault. I'm the one who is obsessed with technology. They're just doing what they see me do. What they don't understand is that when I'm on my devices, most of the time I'm working. But they don't know that; they just know that they want to be on devices like their dad because it's fun!

A couple months ago, I was sitting in church while the sacrament was being administered. Something caught my attention out of the corner of my eye, so I looked over and I saw a very active and faithful adult scrolling through his Facebook newsfeed right during the sacrament prayer. You know the part where it says that we will "always remember Him" (D&C 20:77)? I think it might be close to impossible to focus on the Savior and His sacrifice while you're scrolling through your Facebook feed. Depending on the quality and morality of your friends, you could find yourself in a very precarious situation right during the sacrament. A picture of *xyz* showing up on your newsfeed while the bread is being broken and the prayer is being said is probably not the Savior's idea of respectful. Now if that man has children, and they also scroll through Facebook or Instagram during the sacrament prayer . . . whose fault is it?

We take these devices with us when we go to bed, and we anxiously grab them when we first wake up. We take them into the bathroom with us religiously. (Think about how many times you have talked to someone lately and there was an echo. They were probably in the bathroom.) *Time* just published a statistic that says, "There's a one-in-six chance that your cellphone has fecal matter on it."[2] Remember that the next time your friend hands you their phone. Many of us have panic attacks if we can't find our phones, and we get depressed when the battery runs out. "Those ages 8 to 18 spend more than seven and a half hours a day with such devices," says the *New York Times*.[3] We have them at the dinner table and during movies, and some people can't even get away from them while they're on a date with their spouse.

We don't generally look at our devices as being dangerous to our kids. We let them play with our phones, use their tablets, and download new games on a regular basis because they bug us to death, and we don't want to be mean parents. We also don't want to sit there and listen to them complain that "there's nothing to do;" so we give in and allow them to go into the four corners of the house all by themselves with their own little digital device. We see them stretching their necks because of muscle fatigue and tightness, but we still let them go on. We go back to doing what we were doing and we forget that there's a price tag on the newfound peace and quiet we have just acquired.

We've come to somehow accept unfiltered YouTube videos because it's "just part of the digital age we live in." But holy cow, do you know what can be found on there? We allow our kids to run around with Snapchat—an app built specifically for "sexting."

Snapchat's marketing campaign is aimed toward young teenage girls. How do you feel about that, Dad? It's one of many apps built with the same purpose—to collect information on young people at the expense of their virtue and safety. Did you realize that the Internet security giant McAfee ran a study in 2012 that found that "70 percent of teens hide their online behavior from their parents"?[4] That was in 2012. Snapchat and related apps weren't even invented yet.

I hear teenagers tell me that they leave their headphones in all day while they're in class and that their teachers don't care. Instagram, Facebook, texting, and sexting are what so many kids are "studying" in the age we live in. We even learn how to misspell words so that we can type with our thumbs just a little faster. I have personally met people who don't want to read anymore because "they'd rather watch a video." I actually give that pitch to clients when I'm trying to sell them a corporate video. "People don't want to read anymore," I'll say, "so let's make a video." No one wants to memorize anything anymore because "it's too hard." The loss of concentration, the inability to focus, and the separation anxiety that comes from time away from our devices is subtly dulling and desensitizing our souls.

Brandon Stewart, a Juilliard graduate and one of the founding musical directors for the Millennial Choirs and Orchestras, shared the same sentiment. Brandon and his brother Brett Stewart work with thousands of kids and youth annually in order to produce some of the highest-quality musical masterpieces this world has ever heard. But in my opinion, music is secondary to their real mission. From what I've witnessed, their real purpose is to utilize the discipline and goodness of music to build character in the young men and young women they work with. But the world is not making it easy for the Stewart brothers to accomplish their goals. Brandon shared,

As I work with thousands of youth each year, the biggest concern I have is that I'm seeing a steadily increasing "comatose" state fogging their minds. Ten years ago I would've never thought that in 2016 one of my number one goals working with kids each week would be to wake them up, clear away the foggy layer caused by excessive electronic submersion, and inspire them to become human again—to feel with their souls and spirits, breathe, and connect with other youth face to face. I fear that we have yet to fully realize the severe emotional, spiritual, and physical consequences our youth will experience in coming years due to our overly digital age.[5]

The number of youth that the Stewarts work with is staggering. But to see these musical geniuses fear the overuse and addictive nature of technology above all else is just plain scary.

Don't get me wrong. I'm not a technology hater. I love technology. I built a tech company in college and sold it a few years later to invest and grow other internet-related technology companies. I own an Internet marketing company that specializes in social media.

Technology is my bread and butter, and it's what puts food on our table. But given my background, I've been able to see both sides of tech: the side that makes people and organizations more efficient and the side that is capable of destroying lives—especially young lives. Needless to say, I'm up to my ears in tech, and maybe that's why I am so worried about our society's obsession with it. I've watched people fly to pieces just because their email wasn't working for an hour. I see kids ages eight to eighteen bring it everywhere with them. People and their devices remind me of Gollum from *The Lord of the Rings*. They hold their devices in their hands so tightly and I can almost hear them whispering, "My precious." Try to take it from them and they might even bite your finger off![6] I've seen three-, four-, five-, and six-year-olds that *will not* do anything else but play on an iPad or phone, and then throw a fit if they are denied. Most of the time the parents just give in so that the kids will be quiet. It is the modern-day pacifier for both the young and old, and do you remember how hard it was to wean your infant off that pacifier?

When I was growing up, we were lucky to play a little Atari or Nintendo. Do you remember trying to get your Nintendo to work? Blowing in the games, shaking them, and then hitting the side of the console. There were only a few games too: *Mario Bros.*, *Tecmo Bowl*, *Gyromite*, and *Duck Hunt*. Maybe even a little *Castlevania* or *Metroid* if we were lucky. But the options were limited. We didn't have an endless selection of games just one finger tap away. We'd play them, and we'd get sick of them. But most of the time, we rode bikes, went swimming, and played marbles and pogs. We played hide-and-go-seek, tag, neighborhood-wide kickball, soccer, and many of our own invented games. We were allowed to be bored, and the scarcity of technology forced creativity and out-of-the-box thinking upon us.

The problem is that too many people take their points of view to the extreme. They are either all for technology or completely against it. Smart dads will see that technology is an important part of the world we live in, but, at the same time, they will recognize the difference between using technology to consume mind-numbing, worthless, and addictive materials and using technology to be creative and innovative. You would have never caught Steve Jobs or Bill Gates playing *Pokémon Go* or *Clash of Clans* for hours on end. They were "creating," not "consuming" someone else's creativity.

If my daughter asks me if she can use a video-editing software on the computer so she can edit a family video, I have no problem with her doing so for hours, because she is using her brain in a creative capacity. She is building a skill that can be used throughout her life. Ali Partovi, an advisor to Facebook, Dropbox, and Zappos.com, noted, "Just as I wouldn't dream of limiting how much time a kid can spend with her paintbrushes, or playing her piano, or writing, I think it's absurd to limit her time spent creating computer art, editing video, or computer programming,"[7] When the brain is in creative mode, it's working hard and growing. It will also get fatigued, which will, in turn, force her to want to take a break and do something else. She will come back to it when her brain is rested and she's ready to get back to creating and innovating. But if she was sitting comfortably on the couch with an iPad, consuming the videos or playing any of a seemingly infinite number of addictive games, she could spend an entire day on that device with absolutely nothing to show for it.

When the founders and inventors of the very computers you're working on right now are concerned about the amount of time their own kids spend with the technology they invented, you know there's a problem. Steve Jobs (founder of Apple) and others appear almost as drug dealers who know the dangers of the drug they sell, and therefore take measures to protect their own kids from becoming addicted to it. Even though they know the blessings of the technology, they also know that placing that kind of power without restraint in the hands of their youngsters is one of the most dangerous things they can do.

When journalist Nick Bilton asked Steve Jobs about his children's use of technology at home, the Apple founder blew Nick's mind. Nick assumed that "the Jobs's household was like a nerd's paradise: that the walls were giant touch screens, the dining table was made from tiles of iPads and that iPods were handed out to guests like chocolates on a pillow."[8] Jobs instead told the journalist, "We limit how much technology our kids use at home"[9] and that his kids hadn't even tried using the new iPad.

Nick continued by reporting that this same sentiment was a common theme among many of the chief technology executives and venture capitalists that he had met with. These high-tech dads "strictly limit their children's screen time, often banning all gadgets on school nights, and allocating ascetic time limits on weekends."[10] Nick was confused that tech giants would have such stringent controls on their kids' use of technology while the rest of the world "seem[ed] to take the opposite approach, letting their children bathe in the glow of tablets, smartphones and computers, day and night."[11]

What did these dads know that the rest of the world didn't?

Instead of giving his two boys iPads, Evan Williams, cofounder of Twitter, gives his sons—*gasp*—books. (Like the one you're reading now.) He has tons of them sitting on the shelves for them to read at their will and pleasure. Chris Anderson, former editor of Wired, said there was one rule that was "implemented" by almost all of these high-tech dads: "There are no screens in the bedroom. Period. Ever."[12] These dads are on the front lines and are acutely aware of what goes on with the technology that they invented. Debilitating pornography, bullying, and addiction are all very real and none of these dads want their kids to have any part of it.

Tablets, iPads, phones, and TVs are highly consumable. They're too easy, too comfortable, and too convenient. They are seldom used to build, and instead are primarily used to consume. An adult can use technology wisely to consume information responsibly, but for kids, the danger is too great. If it isn't pornography, it's something else that is calculated to addict. Technology is active vegetation of your kids' minds.

Most dads that I know are into technology. I think that's just the way guys are wired. They love new gadgets, new productivity tools, new games, and anything that they can use to hack a better life for themselves and their families. But we should never let technology get in the way of the relationships we care about the most. Our kids will fight against our desire to limit their technological intake, but they will thank us for it down the road.

NOTES

1. "Nobel Lecture," Christian Lange, *Nobelprize.org*, January 18, 2017.

2. "There's Probably Poop on Your Cellphone," Sam Frizell, *TIME*, January 19, 2017, techland.time.com/2014/01/14/theres-probably-poop-on-your-cellphone.

3. Tamat Lewin, "If Your Kids Are Awake, They're Probably Online," *The New York Times*, January 20, 2010, www.nytimes.com/2010/01/20/education/20wired.html?_r=2&.

4. "70% of Teens Hide Their Online Behavior from Their Parents, McAfee Reveals What U.S. Teens are Really Doing Online, and How Little Their Parents Actually Know," *Intel Security*, January 19, 2017, www.mcafee.com/us/about/news/2012/q2/20120625-01.aspx.

5. Brandon Steward, e-mail correspondence with author, November 26, 2016.

6. *Lord of the Rings: The Return of the King*, directed by Peter Jackson (Burbank, CA: New Line Cinema, 2003), DVD.

7. Ali Partovi quoted in Nick Bilton, "Steve Jobs Was a Low-Tech Parent," *The New York Times*, September 10, 2014, www.nytimes.com/2014/09/11/fashion/steve-jobs-apple-was-a-low-tech-parent.html.

8. Nick Bilton, "Steve Jobs Was a Low-Tech Parent," *The New York Times*, September 10, 2014, www.nytimes.com/2014/09/11/fashion/steve-jobs-apple-was-a-low-tech-parent.html.

9. Steve Jobs quoted in Nick Bilton, "Steve Jobs Was a Low-Tech Parent," *The New York Times*, September 10, 2014, www.nytimes.com/2014/09/11/fashion/steve-jobs-apple-was-a-low-tech-parent.html.

10. Nick Bilton, "Steve Jobs Was a Low-Tech Parent," *The New York Times*, September 10, 2014, www.nytimes.com/2014/09/11/fashion/steve-jobs-apple-was-a-low-tech-parent.html.

11. Ibid.

12. Chris Anderson quoted in Nick Bilton, "Steve Jobs Was a Low-Tech Parent," *The New York Times*, September 10, 2014, www.nytimes.com/2014/09/11/fashion/steve-jobs-apple-was-a-low-tech-parent.html.

SPIRITUAL DADS

DADS WHO
BUILD FORTS

In matters of style, swim with the current; in matters of principle, stand like a rock.

Thomas Jefferson[1]

ABOUT SEVENTY-FIVE YEARS before the time of Christ, Nephite dads built forts to protect their loved ones from their enemies. Captain Moroni was one of those dads. The Book of Mormon says that "if all men had been, and were, and ever would be, like unto Moroni, behold, the very powers of hell would have been shaken forever; yea, the devil would never have power over the hearts of the children of men" (Alma 48:17). That's the kind of dad I want to be. But what exactly did Moroni do to become such a stud? The Book of Mormon gives us his methods for us to use like a blueprint to the lost art of manhood. The method through which he fortified his, and other families, is one which we can apply to our day.

Before Moroni began building forts, he made a declaration to the world that he was going to dedicate his life to protecting the peace and freedom of his family. He wasn't talking only about physical protection; he understood the importance of spiritual protection as well, which is one of the things that made him such an incredible leader and father. Moroni then encouraged people to make covenants with God and to not be ashamed of the gospel of Christ. He reminded them of their ancestors that had gone before and that had sacrificed so much so that they, Moroni's people, could be in the promised land.

But then things started to get really bad. The Lamanites had become committed to wiping Moroni and the Nephites off the face of the earth. So, Moroni went around to his people and did what any good dad would do. The scripture says that Moroni was "preparing the minds of the people to be faithful unto the Lord their God" (Alma 48:7). He prepared the minds of his family and fellow countrymen spiritually before he did anything physically. As we find out later, all of Moroni's efforts to physically prepare his people laid out a pattern for our spiritual preparations.

After Moroni prepared the minds of the people, he began to build little forts as "places of resort" (Alma 48:5). He built walls and other fortifications, and then went around specifically looking for the "weakest fortifications" (Alma 48:9). When he found a weak spot in the fortifications, he doubled his efforts to strengthen that weak spot. Moroni wasn't a procrastinator. He took his role as protector seriously, and he always tried to beat evil invaders to the punch. I believe that there is a direct correlation between a "man who was firm in the faith of Christ" (Alma 48:13) as Moroni was, and a man who builds physical and spiritual forts for his family.

In one of my favorite church manuals, we're reminded that our families have been gathered together into a covenant society in order to "train them to fight evil."[2] Dads today are fighting the same battles that Moroni fought almost two thousand years ago. Only we aren't "throwing up banks of earth" (Alma 48:8) or building physical walls. The forts we build today, as "places of resort," are spiritual in nature. The enemy has become much more intelligent, and instead of charging into our physical fences, he will find ways to infiltrate our forts and cause chaos from within. The forts we build for our families must be even more comprehensive than the Nephite forts of old. Our enemy digs tunnels from below, sends air raids from above, and has the ability to invisibly sneak soul-crushing poison through our walls. Today's enemy knows that if he can destroy us from within, he won't even need to fight us at all. Under his power, our forts will collapse on their own—paving the way for evil to come in and steamroll our families, sending us into oblivion without "root nor branch" (Malachi 4:1).

When we build our forts and put up our fight, we've got to be smart, relentless, and persistent. The forts we build will be inside of our kids; the forts will be a powerful fortress of character that will sustain our kids during troubled times. We need to look for weaknesses in the forts we've already built and strengthen them continually. We can never stop, and we never give in.

NOTES

1. "In matters of style, swim with the current . . . (Quotation)," Thomas Jefferson, *The Jefferson Monticello*, January 18, 2017, www.monticello.org/site/jefferson/matters-style-swim-currentquotation.

2. "Chapter One: Prelude to the Restoration," in *Church History in the Fulness of Times Student Manual* (Salt Lake City: The Church of Jesus Christ of Latter-day Saints, 2003), 1.

DADS WHO PROTECT

Any man who will not fight for
his wife and children is a coward.
Joseph Smith[1]

THERE IS ABSOLUTELY nothing in this world that motivates a good man more than his desire to see his family safe. The mildest of men can turn into the fiercest of lions—stalwartly protecting and defending their families. We can all recall that feeling we get in the pit of our stomach when someone in our family is being attacked. It could be trivial or serious, verbal or physical, but almost everyone has felt that unmistakable feeling at one time or another. It's a feeling that's hard to describe, but you feel like a hulk—an otherwise docile man who turns into an ugly beast without much ability to control it.

While it's important to control these emotions and take a step back before doing something rash, it's also important to understand that these emotions are not bad. The emotions that we feel as a dad are godly emotions, given to us as a means of providing protection and security for our families in all aspects of their lives. Being a protector is so much more than being a tough guy in the middle of the night when someone is trying to break into your house. It's about protecting your family from any and all threats that might impact their happiness.

Many people today only think of Jesus Christ as being the kind, meek, miracle worker who was nice to everyone. While all of that is true about Christ, we sometimes forget that He was referenced six times in the Bible as "El-kana" or a "jealous God."[2] We sometimes wonder how it is that God can be jealous, but it's not the act of jealousy that is being conveyed by using the Hebrew word for "jealousy" in the scriptures. It's the emotion associated with the act of jealousy that is at the heart of the description. "The Semitic root קנא (*qn'*) appears to denote a becoming deep red."[3] That red emotion in the Hebrew is associated with the deepest levels of love and hate. Sometimes we describe ourselves as "seeing red" when we're in protection mode for our families.

Our eldest brother Jesus was in protection mode over His family while in the garden, and He will be in protection mode again as He returns to the earth once more. When He returns to this earth, He will not be returning as a lamb, and He won't be wearing white as depicted in some images. Christ returns to protect us as a lion—His eyes "as a flame of fire" (Revelation 19:12)—and He will be wearing red according to the book of Revelation (Revelation 19:11–13). His love for us, in its purest form, always manifested itself in red: blood red in the garden and blood red in His raiment upon His eventual return to protect and defend us from our attackers. What the scriptures describe as jealousy is really just an attempt to describe Jesus's godly desire to protect and defend those that He calls His. That "kana" or "qana"[4] that we see in Christ is an attribute that is hardwired into every dad that holds his child for the first time. Dads have been given that "kana"—that fire, that love, that protection, that devotion—and it can only be described as a godly emotion.

In a blog entry to some of her girlfriends, my wife elaborated on her desire to have a protective dad and husband in her home. She said,

> All women want a strong man who can protect the family from an intruder in the home. A manly man who can beat off a pack of starving wolves to save his family. But what I am talking about runs deeper. The man I'm talking about needs to be not only the protector of the physical needs of the family but also a protector of the spiritual and emotional needs of your family. A man who is a protector of the spiritual needs of his family thinks it essential to pray and read scriptures together. He is a good teacher as well as example of all that is good in manhood so that your children can see a stark contrast between the outside world and your home. He is stalwart and faithful in all his duties and reliable. A man who is a protector of the emotional needs of his family speaks kindly, forgives easily and is not too prideful to say he is sorry. His physical protection pales in comparison to the spiritual protection he brings to the home. I don't know about you, but the home I want to create for my children is a safe, nurturing environment that is a refuge from the storms of the outside world. If this is the kind of home you want to create, make sure you find a man who wants to create the same environment for his family and is willing to man-up to the responsibility and not just leave it up to you.[5]

What my wife is saying here echoes a quote from Elder Holland that was stated in an earlier chapter in this book: "Of even greater concern than the physical absenteeism of some fathers is the spiritually or emotionally absent father."[6] My wife believes that we should treat spiritual and emotional threats to our families with the same seriousness and urgency that we might treat physical threats or attacks. We would never just stand by and let someone hurt our family physically, and yet, so many men stand by and watch the spiritual and emotional darts of Satan descend upon their family without blinking an eye. This same sentiment is shared by the Savior as He expressed more worry and concern about those things that might destroy our souls over those that might hurt our bodies. (See Matthew 10:28.)

Pornography is a prime example of something that persistently attacks the spiritual and emotional aspects of a family. It has subtly become the most destructive weapon on earth against the family. It's a masked monster, a Trojan horse, and a destroyer of everything that is pure. It's claiming victims and wiping out the moral compass of millions of people worldwide. It alone has been the root cause of some of the basest crimes ever committed against the young and the innocent. It alone can destroy the expectations of men, the beauty of women, and the romance that could exist between the two. Elder Dallin H. Oaks said, "Evil that used to be localized and covered like a boil is now legalized and paraded like a banner. . . . The movies and magazines and television [and I might add the Internet] that shape our attitudes are filled with stories or images that portray the children of God as predatory beasts or, at best, as trivial creations pursuing little more than personal pleasure. And too many of us accept this as entertainment."[7]

"Accidental" children out of wedlock is the norm. Abortions are the norm. People have been desensitized and animalized, and the family unit has been decimated. Pornography, which might be the most dangerous addiction this earth has ever seen, is now accessible to children and adults of all ages. Smartphones provide one-click access to the dirtiest things the human mind can conjure up. In 1986, the FBI interviewed thirty-six major serial killers. Based on those interviews, the Attorney General's Commission declared that 81 percent of the killers that were studied said "their biggest sexual interest was in reading pornography."[8] Ted Bundy, one of the most recognized serial killers in human history said in his final interview before being executed that his early exposure to pornography is what sent him in the direction of acting out "the fantasies he had seen depicted for so long."[9] Another serial killer by the name of Arthur Bishop (who was executed for sodomizing and murdering five boys ages four to thirteen), said these words regarding pornography: "Pornography wasn't the only negative influence in my life, but its effect on me was devastating. I lost all sense of decency and respect for humanity and life, and I would do anything or take any risk to fulfill my deviant desires."[10]

Both of these men described their addictions as starting with "soft" or common pornography. Then they sought for harder stuff until their addiction became so uncontrollable that they had to act out the things they were seeing. It lulled them in, bound them softly, then locked them up. Once this monster had them, he turned them into puppets of devastation.

These are extreme cases. I understand that. But pornography leads to the destruction of one of humanity's greatest gifts. Devastation is taking place all over the world on a micro and macro scale because of a disregard for marriage, fidelity, responsibility, and loyalty. The world is suffering from a shortage of true love, and dads everywhere need to band together to protect and fight against this evil that attacks the spiritual and emotional fortifications of our families.

Kids can watch this stuff on their devices at any given time. Then, they ignorantly create their own porn. Boys turn girls into sex objects by seventh or eighth grade. Those girls then find themselves at the abortion clinic, scarred for life, while the boy has moved on to "someone with less baggage." It's sad and sickening to see what people are going through because of this plague. Using technology, young kids ask for naked pictures and attempt to recreate the scenarios they see on their devices. They don't need to be eighteen anymore or sneak into an adult video store. All they have to do is type a few words into Google and it's there: the most degrading and debilitating drug known to mankind. It is consumed almost immediately. There is no smoke, no needle, no smell, and no money required. It's just there. The result is an estimated 125,000 abortions performed each day, or 40 to 50 million abortions performed each year with an associated boatload of despair.

Moms everywhere wish it would just go away and stop ruining their lives. They want protectors who will step up and fight against it, and who will then teach their kids to abolish it from their lives. They're pleading with us to stand up and fight for them in a world that is consistently threatening to diminish and destroy their virtue and goodness. This is just one of many examples in which a dad can be the "protector of all that is sacred": by intelligently and tenaciously fighting against the spiritual and emotional attacks that are being hurled against his family.[11]

NOTES

1. "Journal, December 1842–June 1844; Book 1, 21 December 1842–10 March 1843," *The Joseph Smith Papers*, accessed January 18, 2017, 162; www.josephsmithpapers.org/paper -summary/journal-december-1842-june-1844-book-1-2 -december-1842-10-march-1843/170

2. "El-kana meaning," *Abarim Publications*, January 18, 2017, www.abarim-publications.com/Meaning/El-kana.html#.WH _wMmTytz8.

3. Ibid.

4. Ibid.

5. Kristyn Trimble, "5 Ways You Know You've Found the 'Right Man'," *GregTrimble.com*, www.gregtrimble.com/5-ways-you -know-youve-found-the-right-man.

6. Jeffrey R. Holland, "The Hands of the Fathers," *Ensign*, May 1999.

7. Dallin H. Oaks, "Preparation for the Second Coming," *Ensign*, May 2004.

8. Jerry Kirk, "Ted Bundy Shows Us the Crystallizing Effects of Pornography," *Los Angeles Times*, February 8, 1989, articles .latimes.com/1989-02-08/local/me-1969_1_ted-bundy.

9. Ibid.

10. Ibid.

11. Kristyn Trimble, "5 Ways You Know You've Found the 'Right Man'," *GregTrimble.com*, www.gregtrimble.com/5-ways-you -know-youve-found-the-right-man.

DADS WHO FACE TRIALS

It's not what happens to you, but how you react to it that matters.

Epictetus[1]

MOST PEOPLE CAN'T remember what they were doing on March 6, 2006. But for my friend and his family, that day will forever be remembered as the day their lives were turned completely upside down. Jon and Christina Hales were going about their lives—living the dream. They had been married for ten years and had four beautiful daughters. They had been discussing how smooth their life had been over the years and were grateful for their good fortune.

Jon was an art director for well-known video game development companies, including Midway, EA, and Disney. He worked long hours and had a tough commute but still found ways to be an amazing dad. According to his wife, Christina, Jon would "get up in the mornings, teach [the kids] how to make breakfast, and then drop them off for school before heading into work,"[2] so that she could get an extra hour of sleep. At night, he would "gather all of them on his back and give them horseback rides up the stairs into bed. He would tell them stories, but use their names spelled backwards as the characters' names. He would take them on wild adventures that he would make up on the spot."[3] Jon was a strong, able, and energetic dad.

Being a dad and a family man was everything to Jon, so he decided to take a risk and venture out by starting a new business, in order to have more time to spend at home with his family. After about a year of building this business, Jon was ready to launch and present his new idea at a conference. Just two days before the conference, Jon went out to ride dirt bikes with a couple of friends. Jon wasn't doing anything crazy out there that day. He was just cruising along when he hit a dip that happened to have a rock in it. When his front tire went into the dip, the tire bounced off of the rock and projected him over the handlebars. The result was an obliterated C5 and a bruised spinal cord. In a split second, Jon—this strong, energetic stud of a dad—lost the ability to give his daughters anymore horseback rides. Jon was now a quadriplegic.

Jon spent the next three days in the ICU, the following four days in a regular hospital bed, and then nine weeks in rehab. Life, according to Christina, "went from calm, casual, and carefree, to chaotic, stressful, and sleepless."[4] Things would never be the same for their family. I can imagine that Jon lay there thinking about one thing more than any other: "How am I going to be a dad to my family?"

The next year for Jon was incredibly hard. His nerve endings were misfiring, which caused a lot of physical pain. He went from taking care of people to being taken care of. But it was the mental torment that surely outweighed anything physical. Jon could have thrown in the towel. He could have wallowed in permanent despair, and no one would have judged him for it. He could have worn a frown, and we all would've understood why.

At a stakewide temple trip, my wife came in contact with Jon for the first time. At the time, she didn't know him or his story. She spent that entire session crying because of one thing: "There was a man in the back of the session who was bound to a wheelchair and seemed to be having a hard time," she explained. But it wasn't the fact that he was having a hard time that was causing such emotions to swell within her. "It was the perpetual smile on his face" that pierced her soul in the midst of that holy house. She said that this man maintained a smile unlike any she had ever seen. He could easily justify staying home and not participating. It melted her heart as she thought of what this man had to go through and what he is still going through, and yet here he was, dedicated, committed, and beaming in the temple! She could see the enabling power of the Atonement radiating from him as he sat there with a smile that seemed as permanent as the chair he was in.[5]

Jon's wife, Christina, said that as Jon lost the use of his arms and legs, his heart simultaneously grew "tenfold."[6] What Jon lacked in physical abilities was now overshadowed by the abundance of spiritual attributes that manifested themselves as the years went by. Now he "rolls down the hallway to have one-on-one chats with his daughters." He cruises down the street to the yogurt shop for a small treat with them. He attends their sporting events and "cheers so hard that he almost falls out of his chair with excitement."[7] All of this Jon does with a smile.

Mentally, spiritually, and emotionally, Jon stayed around to fight. With the never-ending support of a loving God, a faithful wife, and the image of his precious children burned into his heart, he found a way to be a fountain for his family and to the world.

Life has a way of being really, really good—and then really, really bad—really, really fast. It can happen to any of us, at any time, without much effort at all on our part. We have no idea when it's coming, how it's coming, or even if it's coming. It can happen to good people or bad people, and it can appear to be without any rhyme or reason. But a real man, and a real dad, will take his circumstance for what it is and make lemonade from his lemons—no matter how sour they might be.

NOTES

1. "Epictetus: Quotable Quote," *Goodreads*, January 20, 2017, www.goodreads.com/quotes/239288-it-s-not-what-happens -to-you-but-how-you-react.
2. Christina Hales, personal correspondence with author.
3. Ibid.
4. Ibid.
5. Kristyn Trimble, personal correspondence with author.
6. Christina Hales, personal correspondence with author.
7. Ibid.

PUT THE LORD FIRST

DADS WHO LEAVE A LEGACY

Carve your name on hearts, not tombstones.
A legacy is etched into the minds of others
and the stories they share about you.
Shannon L. Alder[1]

I RECENTLY SAT down to meet with the CEO and the IT director of a company that was interested in hiring my company for services related to our digital agency. This was a massive three hundred million dollar company—an industry leader in Southern California. As the meeting went on, we began discussing their social media presence and subsequently brought up their Facebook page. One lone face popped up on the side of the screen showing me that I had a mutual friend that liked this company's Facebook page. That man was Daniel Rasmussen. The CEO immediately noted Daniel's face, causing me to ask, "Do you know Daniel Rasmussen?"

The CEO answered, "Yeah, Daniel is a great guy! He was our attorney. He left to go on some kind of mission thing," I cracked a smile, as I already knew that Daniel had been called to serve as a mission president in Peru. I was grateful to have the opportunity to confirm the goodness of Daniel, and also share that I too had served a mission for that same church.

As I thought about it later, I considered how huge it was that Daniel Rasmussen had willingly left revenue from companies like this during the peak earning years of his career in order to answer the call to serve a mission in a third-world country for the span of three years. But that was just the beginning of the type of sacrifices he'd have to make along the way.

I saw Daniel Rasmussen's son, Danny, post a few pictures of his sister's wedding online, and noticed that they were carrying around a picture of his dad's face on a poster board. I wondered what in the world was going on. I asked Danny for a little background on the situation. In his own words, he describes how they arrived at that day without having his dad there with them:

> My baby sister Camille is nine years younger than me, the next closest sibling, and has in some respects been raised as though she were an only child. She's always been close with my parents as a result. When the time came for her to decide to serve a mission, she enthusiastically submitted her papers and received a call to serve in the Peru Chiclayo Mission in Northern Peru. Not too long into her mission, my dad received a call from the Office of Elder Quentin L. Cook to schedule a Skype session with the Apostle. Since his dad had served as a mission president, my dad knew what this likely meant: it was possible that he would be asked to leave his full-time job in comfortable Orange County, California, to dedicate three years to the Lord serving as a mission president. A few weeks later, they accepted the call to serve during a Skype session with President Uchtdorf. Though they did not yet know where they would be serving for several months, they were excited with the prospect of going on this adventure together.

When the letter finally came, they opened it in eager anticipation only to discover that they would be serving in the Peru Piura Mission—the mission directly north of Camille's mission in Chiclayo.

Over the next year, Camille became an important anchor for my parents, especially my mother, who needed someone who knew what it was like to live in obscure Northern Peru. She primed them on what they could expect for life in Peru: the weather, the food, the people, the culture, and even what shoes to wear. Camille ultimately finished her mission in Peru, came home, and met a wonderful young man just a few weeks after returning from her mission. She fell in love and prepared to get married just six months later—just thirteen months into my parent's mission.

Of course, the nature of the assignment is such that it is more than a full-time job. It's an all-your-time job—morning, noon and night. For my dad, it meant not leaving the borders of his mission for three whole years, while my mom wouldn't be able to come home for anything save it be for the death or marriage of one of her children. Seeing as Camille was the only one of the kids not yet married, my parents braced themselves for the possibility that, should Camille decide to get married during their three years in Peru, my parents would miss all the wedding planning, and my dad would miss the wedding itself, as well.

This proved to be an easier sacrifice in theory than it came to be in reality. My mom flew home for the wedding week and all was well, but when the big day came, our entire family felt the gaping hole in the center of our family. After all, the sealing is about forging family bonds that last forever, and in that room, each of us wanted was to have him there with us too. I sat in his chair and witnessed the ordinance on his behalf, looking into the eyes of my little sister as she knelt across the altar with the light of Christ beaming from her face. This sight wasn't mine to behold. It belonged to my dad and it stung that he wasn't here to witness it himself.

The sacrifice is always easier in theory, but when the full gravity of that sacrifice bears down upon us, that's when the promised blessings begin to flow. After the sealing, we dragged my dad around all day long in the form of a cardboard cutout and a face trying not to show his tears through FaceTime on his iPhone. We would have loved to have him physically with us that day, but we all knew that he made the right choice.

That's my dad. He's the guy who has given himself over completely to the service of the Lord. He trusts Him, and teaches us every day through his example that as we put the Lord first in our lives, all will work out just as it should.[2]

As I listen to my friend describe his faithful dad, I can't help but think of the righteously famous two thousand young warriors who fought to protect the freedom of their families and their country. For years, I never even considered that so many of these young men grew up without a dad, and why it had to be so. The dads of these young men were converts of the great missionary Ammon, and had come to be known as the Anti-Nephi-Lehies or the "people of Ammon" (Alma 43:11). These were the fiercest of Lamanites who, upon conversion, made a covenant and promise with God that they would never shed blood again. Their covenant with God was put to the test when other, unconverted Lamanites came to fight and kill the Anti-Nephi-Lehies because of their conversion to the gospel and their association with the Nephites. Can you imagine the scene of death that took place as these faithful Lamanite converts buried their weapons and subsequently bowed their heads to the ground as they were slaughtered without contest? Their faith was so deep, their conversion so solid, and their love of God so strong that they were willing to give up their lives to keep their covenants.

Three major things happened as a result of these brave converts who kept their covenants.

First, when the Lamanites began to slaughter their brethren and realized that their victims wouldn't fight back, it caused them to stop, admire, and repent of what they were doing. The record says that "there were many whose hearts had swollen in them for those of their brethren who had fallen under the sword, for they repented of the things which they had done" (Alma 24:24). The net result of this situation was that those Lamanites who came to kill these converts ultimately became converts themselves. It was said that more Lamanites joined the Church that day than the number of converts who were killed.

Second, the wives of these Anti-Nephi-Lehi men who made covenants with God stood by and watched their husbands submit to their aggressors and lose their lives. These women were probably already great mothers, but this act of covenant keeping surely endeared them even more to their late husbands and solidified their faith in God. They didn't look upon their husbands as cowards who would not fight. Rather, they must have considered them more courageous than they had ever been in any of their previous battles. The blood they gave must have been held as a sacred symbol of their devotion to God. These women eventually become one of the crowing jewels of the Book of Mormon, and are legendary mothers among all Latter-day Saints. The remaining living Anti-Nephi-Lehies—which included these mothers—were "distinguished for their zeal towards God, and also towards men; for they were perfectly honest and upright in all things; and they were firm in the faith of Christ, even unto the end" (Alma 27:27).

Third, the young sons of these men also had to stand by and helplessly watch their dads be savagely taken from this earth. Sadly, they had to watch and learn through the shedding of blood just how important God was to their dads. While there could have been many other lessons these dads could have taught their sons had they remained on the earth a little longer, no lesson could have been as impactful and convincing than what they witnessed on that fateful day. Phillip Brooks once observed, "How carefully most men creep into nameless graves, while now and again one or two forget themselves into immortality."[3] The dad who maintains his integrity, sets the example, and tenaciously lives what he believes, is the dad who leaves the biggest mark on the future spiritual and temporal success of those that come after him. These dads become immortal in the lives of their wife and kids, as well as the lines of posterity that look toward their ancestors for guidance.

NOTES

1. Pastor Stephen Kyeyune, *The Legacy of a Hero: Life Lived from the Christian Perspective* (Bloomington, IN: AuthorHouse, 2014), 214.
2. Danny Rasmussen, personal correspondence with author.
3. Phillip Brooks quoted in Gordon B. Hinckley, "Forget Yourself," *BYU Speeches*, March 6, 1977.

DADS WHO CELEBRATE

*Don't save something only
for a special occasion. Every day
in your life is a special occasion.*
Thomas S. Monson[1]

ONE OF THE most important things that Heavenly Father implemented from the Creation of the world was the concept of a celebration. As God was wrapping up the Creation of our world, He took a break from His labors on the seventh day and called it the Sabbath. It was known to all of God's children as a "day of rest." (See Exodus 34:21.) For many of us, that day has become an obligatory day of boredom and solemnity.

But what many people don't realize, is that this was never God's intention for the Sabbath. This day was meant to be a day in which Heavenly Father gathered His children together to celebrate and commemorate the great things they had accomplished during the week. Our Heavenly Father likes to celebrate! And we should too!

We should enthusiastically find things to celebrate about with our families, and we should do it as often as we can! We should find reasons to commemorate special events, and if the special events are few and far between, then we should make more special events— and then celebrate those. These celebrations, according to my friend John Dye, will be the "familial glue that bonds you together during the tough times."[2]

The concept of familial glue and bonding is central to the purpose of our Heavenly Father's desire to celebrate. He likes to celebrate so much that he made it a commandment for us to celebrate at least once a week. The Sabbath, from the beginning of our world, was meant to be a day of celebration—not a day to lie in our beds with the doors closed and the lights off for the rest of the day after church.

"Resting" is relative to our definition of rest. Did God "rest" from His labors on the Sabbath day because He was tired? Do we think that God can even get tired? Does anyone really believe that when God "rested" from His labors on the seventh day, that He went and found a cloudy recliner in some faraway galaxy to isolate Himself on for the afternoon?

In Genesis 2, when it says that God "rested" from His labors, the Hebrew lexicon defines "rest" as something very different from what we might take it for in the English. Two Hebrew definitions stuck out to me: "repose,"[3] which in the English was defined as "peace" and "tranquility,"[4] as well as "to celebrate."[5]

Nowhere, in the various contexts and definitions of the Sabbath, have I found the concept of sleeping or idleness to be what the Lord intended us to do with that day. In fact, it seems to be quite the opposite. I'm not saying that taking a nap on the Sabbath is bad, but what I am saying is that the Sabbath was meant for so much more.

The Sabbath day commandment is interesting because you think, "It's just a day of the week—what's the big deal? Why is it one of the big ten commandments, and why do modern apostles focus on this seemingly ancillary commandment so persistently?"

My personal belief is that the primary purpose of the Sabbath is to preserve the "religion of our families." The word "religion" comes from the Latin *religare* which means "to bind."[6] (Remember the familial glue that bonds us together during tough times?) The Sabbath has always been thought of as the day in which we "get religion," but if we take the true meaning of religion as our guide, then the Sabbath is actually a day set apart for us "to bind" with our families.

If I had to guess what topic the apostles and prophets are most concerned about in these last days, I might guess that it would have something to do with preserving families from this final onslaught. What is the best way to go about preserving and protecting families? The answer: to bind ourselves together on the Sabbath!

Elder Christofferson has spoken in the past about focusing on desired outcomes,[7] and in my mind, the most desirable outcome for the Sabbath is that we would come together and bind ourselves back to each other with Christ's Atonement at the center of those activities. The Atonement is the ultimate reconciliation, binding, and sealing agent. It is at the heart of pure religion.

Pure religion, as James defines it, is to "visit the fatherless and the widows" and to "keep [yourself] unspotted from the world" (James 1:27).

Why the fatherless and the widows? Because they lack family members to bind (*religare*) with and derive strength from. That is why we come together on Sundays: to be with and strengthen both our immediate and ward families.

How do we keep ourselves unspotted from the world? The Lord tells us in the Doctrine and Covenants, "And that thou mayest more fully keep thyself unspotted from the world, thou shalt go to the house of prayer and offer up thy sacraments upon my holy day" (D&C 59:9). Pure religion, then, is the act of preserving families through the application of the Atonement of Christ. For us, almost all of this takes place on Sunday.

Each major Sabbath day from the beginning of time, and throughout the ages, has been because there has been an act of grace worth celebrating. The Creation of the earth, the Exodus (God's deliverance of His people out of bondage in Egypt), the Resurrection of Jesus Christ—all of these events revolved around one concept: the deliverance, preservation, and progression of God's covenant families. That is a concept worth celebrating!

As a dad, the Sabbath has been something that has nagged at me for many years. It's always bugged me because I never had a hard-and-fast rule to determine whether what I was doing on the Sabbath was right or wrong for my family. But I've finally come up with a rule that brings peace to my mind for any and every Sabbath activity:

Always make sacrifices that strengthen your relationship with God and your family. You know you're violating the Sabbath if you are making sacrifices that weaken those relationships.

Easy.

When I apply that rule to each Sabbath activity, I find peace, tranquility, and a cause to celebrate. To paraphrase Elder Bednar's words, the Sabbath becomes like a cool drink of water after a hot day of working in the sun.[8]

The Father we all aspire to become like chose to implement a plan whereby we would be reminded to celebrate our families. He wants us to celebrate our accomplishments and, most importantly, our relationship with God on a regular basis. The things we celebrate often turn into traditions, and traditions create some of the fondest memories a child can have.

So dads! Celebrate! By all means, find things to celebrate!

NOTES

1. Thomas S. Monson, "In Search of Treasure," *Ensign*, May 2003.
2. John Dye, Facebook correspondence with author.
3. *Strong's Exhaustive Concordance of the Bible*, s.v., "H7673 shabath," www.blueletterbible.org/lang/lexicon/lexicon.cfm?Strongs=H7673&t=KJV.
4. *Merriam-Webster*, s.v., "repose," noun, January 19, 2017, www.merriam-webster.com/dictionary/repose.
5. *Strong's Exhaustive Concordance of the Bible*, s.v., "H7673 shabath," www.blueletterbible.org/lang/lexicon/lexicon.cfm?Strongs=H7673&t=KJV.
6. *Online Etymology Dictionary*, s.v., "religion," January 19, 2017, www.etymonline.com/index.php?term=religion.
7. D. Todd Christofferson in "October 2015: Sabbath Day Observance," 5:20 (general conference leadership meeting, October 2015), www.lds.org/broadcasts/archive/general-conference-leadership-training/2015/10.
8. David A. Bednar in "October 2015: Sabbath Day Observance," 2:45 (general conference leadership meeting, October 2015), www.lds.org/broadcasts/archive/general-conference-leadership-training/2015/10.

DAD'S GREATEST JOY

The happiest moments of my life
have been the few which I have passed
at home in the bosom of my family.
Thomas Jefferson[1]

I RECENTLY SAT in a church planning meeting where I quietly asked the guy to the left of me and the guy to the right of me what their greatest joy would be as a father. I then followed up by mentally placing them in a scenario in which they are lying on their beds with one or two days to live. I asked them to describe to me what would bring peace to their mind as a father before they passed.

The man on my right said that his greatest joy would be for him to have "stayed close to his children during adulthood." He didn't elaborate, but he didn't have to. I understood exactly what he was talking about. One of my deepest desires in life is that I will have strong relationships with my kids, and that those relationships will endure beyond the first twenty years of their life. I want to be there for them as they move into their various adult stages. I want to be there for them, and I want them to want to be there for me. Too many men lose contact with their kids once their kids turn into adults—possibly because of strained relationships during the teenage years or for other reasons. It's sad to see twenty years of being around a child everyday turn into seeing them once every five years.

In times past, family members would stay close together in order to provide support to one another. Now, it seems as if children can't wait to get as far away from their parents as possible. I know that society has changed and that jobs are offered far from home. I know that some opportunities result in children moving away, but I believe that if we can put in the time and effort when our children are young, that they will have a desire to stay close to us as parents as the years go by.

The man to the left of me had a similar answer to my initial question. He told me that his greatest joy as a dad "evolves over time" and will change with different stages of his life: to see them go on missions, get married in the temple, and ultimately keep their faith later in life. He said that these stages were stepping-stones, even milestones that contribute to his deepest desire to have his children with him in the eternities. He told me that his dad had a saying in their home, and he has adopted it in his: "No empty chairs."

Almost every good dad ultimately wants the same thing. He wants to see his children learn and grow and develop into marvelous adults. He wants to see them grow up and fight for their families. He wants to see them live up to their divine potential. He wants to hear stories of how his children lift and bless others. As the Apostle John said, "[good dads] have no greater joy than to hear that [their] children walk in truth" (3 John 1:4).

When the great prophet Lehi was about to die, he gathered his children together to give them some final advice. Of all the things he could have chosen to say to them, he spent the final moments of his life by testifying of the Savior. He said, "I would that ye should look to the great Mediator, and hearken unto his great commandments; and be faithful unto his words" (2 Nephi 2:28). Lehi then emphasized to his family that we have the ability to "choose" to be happy or miserable. Lehi pled with his children to "choose" happiness. And that is a father's greatest joy! To see his children "choose" happiness over misery. Lehi explained, "I have none other object save it be the everlasting welfare of your souls" (2 Nephi 2:30). That was Lehi's priority. He lived his life for his family, and protected them physically and spiritually by relying on God during troubled times.

Everything that I do, everything that I am, and everything that I want to be, is for my family. I believe that God placed me on this earth to watch over and protect them first and foremost. Everything else that I might do in this life pales in comparison to my responsibility to fight for them in a world that is trying to tear us apart. Our hearts can't fail us now. We've got to be dads who stay and fight!

NOTES

1. "Extract from Thomas Jefferson to Francis Willis," Thomas Jefferson, *The Jefferson Monticello*, January 20, 2017, tjrs.monticello.org/letter/127.

ABOUT THE AUTHOR

GREG TRIMBLE IS an Internet blogger who has reached millions of people around the world through his writings. He is the CEO of Yalla—an online team management and project collaboration application. He's also the founder of Lemonade Stand—a digital marketing agency located in Southern California.

Greg's articles have been picked up and syndicated by major news outlets around the country. He speaks nationally to various congregations about the power of the Internet and social media in sharing the gospel of The Church of Jesus Christ of Latter-day Saints. He has a passion for the logic and beauty of the gospel and has taught as an institute and seminary teacher for six years.

Greg loves to surf, play golf, and, above all else, hang out with his wife, Kristyn, and his two kids, Taylor and Trenton.

Scan to visit

www.gregtrimble.com